James

Faith at Work

Group Directory

Pass this Directory around and have your Group Members
fill in their names and phone numbers

Name   **Phone**

_____   _____

_____   _____

_____   _____

_____   _____

_____   _____

_____   _____

_____   _____

_____   _____

_____   _____

_____   _____

_____   _____

_____   _____

_____   _____

James

EDITING AND PRODUCTION TEAM:

James F. Couch, Jr., Lyman Coleman, Sharon Penington, Katharine Harris, Ashley Benedict, Christopher Werner, Matthew Lockhart, Richard Peace, Cathy Tardif, Andrew Sloan, Scott Lee, Gregory C. Benoit, Erika Tiepel

NASHVILLE, TENNESSEE

Published by Serendipity House Publishers
Nashville, Tennessee

International Standard Book Number: 1-57494-330-8

ACKNOWLEDGMENTS

Scripture quotations are taken from the Holman Christian Standard Bible,
© Copyright 2000 by Holman Bible Publishers. Used by permission.

Nashville, Tennessee
1-800-525-9563
www.serendipityhouse.com

Table of Contents

Core Values

Community: The purpose of this curriculum is to build community within the body of believers around Jesus Christ.

Group Process: To build community, the curriculum must be designed to take a group through a step-by-step process of sharing your story with one another.

Interactive Bible Study: To share your "story," the approach to Scripture in the curriculum needs to be open-ended and right brain—to "level the playing field" and encourage everyone to share.

Developmental Stages: To provide a healthy program throughout the four stages of the life cycle of a group, the curriculum needs to offer courses on three levels of commitment: (1) Beginner Level—low-level entry, high structure, to level the playing field; (2) Growth Level—deeper Bible study, flexible structure, to encourage group accountability; (3) Discipleship Level—in-depth Bible study, open structure, to move the group into high gear.

Target Audiences: To build community throughout the culture of the church, the curriculum needs to be flexible, adaptable and transferable into the structure of the average church.

Mission: To expand the Kingdom of God one person at a time by filling the "empty chair." (We add an extra chair to each group session to remind us of our mission.)

Introduction

Each healthy small group will move through various stages as it matures.

Multiply Stage: The group begins the multiplication process. Members pray about their involvement in new groups. The "new" groups begin the life cycle again with the Birth Stage.

Birth Stage: This is the time in which group members form relationships and begin to develop community. The group will spend more time in ice-breaker exercises, relational Bible study and covenant building.

Develop Stage: The inductive Bible study deepens while the group members discover and develop gifts and skills. The group explores ways to invite their neighbors and coworkers to group meetings.

Growth Stage: Here the group begins to care for one another as it learns to apply what they learn through Bible study, worship and prayer.

Subgrouping: If you have nine or more people at a meeting, Serendipity recommends you divide into subgroups of 3–6 for the Bible study. Ask one person to be the leader of each subgroup and to follow the directions for the Bible study. After 30 minutes, the Group Leader will call "time" and ask all subgroups to come together for the Caring Time.

Each group meeting should include all parts of the "three-part agenda."

 Ice-Breaker: Fun, history-giving questions are designed to warm the group and to build understanding about the other group members. You can choose to use all of the Ice-Breaker questions, especially if there is a new group member that will need help in feeling comfortable with the group.

 Bible Study: The heart of each meeting is the reading and examination of the Bible. The questions are open, discover questions that lead to further inquiry. Reference notes are provided to give everyone a "level playing field." The emphasis is on understanding what the Bible says and applying the truth to real life. The questions for each session build. There is always at least one "going deeper" question provided. You should always leave time for the last of the "questions for interaction." Should you choose, you can use the optional "going deeper" question to satisfy the desire for the challenging questions in groups that have been together for a while.

 Caring Time: All study should point us to actions. Each session ends with prayer and direction in caring for the needs of the group members. You can choose between several questions. You should always pray for the "empty chair." Who do you know that could fill that void in your group?

Sharing Your Story: These sessions are designed for members to share a little of their personal lives each time. Through a number of special techniques, each member is encouraged to move from low risk, less personal sharing to higher risk responses. This helps develop the sense of community and facilitates caregiving.

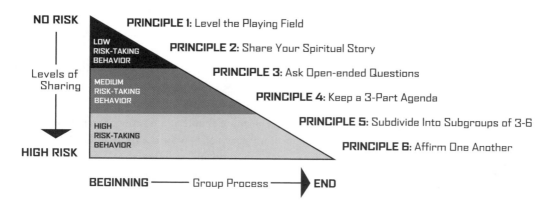

Group Covenant: A group covenant is a "contract" that spells out your expectations and the ground rules for your group. It's very important that your group discuss these issues—preferably as part of the first session.

Ground Rules:

- Priority: While you are in the group, you give the group meeting priority.

- Participation: Everyone participates and no one dominates.

- Respect: Everyone is given the right to their own opinion and all questions are encouraged and respected.

- Confidentiality: Anything that is said in the meeting is never repeated outside the meeting.

- Empty Chair: The group stays open to new people at every meeting.

- Support: Permission is given to call upon each other in time of need—even in the middle of the night.

- Advice Giving: Unsolicited advice is not allowed.

- Mission: We agree to do everything in our power to start a new group as our mission.

Issues:

- The time and place this group is going to meet is _____.

- Refreshments are _____ responsibility.

- Child care is _____ responsibility.

SESSION 1
Consider it Joy
SCRIPTURE JAMES 1:1–11

Welcome

Welcome to this study of the book of James. In the sessions to follow we will be exploring James' practical instructions for the Christian life. We will have the opportunity to learn and grow together as a group as we seek to apply what we hear from God's Word.

The author has traditionally been assumed to be James, the leader of the church in Jerusalem and the brother of Jesus (Mark 6:3). We know that James was a strict Jew who adhered to the Mosaic Law (Gal. 2:12), yet unlike the Judaizers, he supported Paul's ministry to the Gentiles (Acts 21:17–26). Later accounts indicate that James was martyred in A.D. 62. The question of who wrote the book of James is still, however, somewhat of a puzzle, primarily because Jesus and his saving work is mentioned so little—a curious omission if the author was Jesus' brother. This question baffled even the ancient church. Both the Latin Father Jerome and the church historian Eusebius observe that not all accept James as having been written by our Lord's brother.

Among the New Testament books, James is an oddity. It is written in quite a different style from the others, more like the book of Proverbs than Paul's epistles. But even more than its style, its contents set James apart. It does not cover many of the topics we have come to expect in the New Testament. There is no mention of the Holy Spirit and no reference to the redemptive work or resurrection of Christ. In fact, it contains only two references to the name of Jesus Christ (1:1; 2:1). Furthermore, when examples are given, they are drawn from the lives of Old Testament prophets, not from the experiences of Jesus. Although the title *Lord* appears 11 times, it generally refers to the name of God and not to Jesus. Indeed, it is God the Father who is the focus in the book of James.

While James clearly stands in the tradition of other Christian writers, he has some special concerns. The relationship between rich and poor comes up at various points (1:9–11; 5:1–4)—an issue of special significance to the modern affluent West. He is concerned about the use and abuse of speech (1:19,22–24,26; 2:12; 3:3–12; 5:12). He gives instruction on prayer (1:5–8; 4:2–3; 5:13–18). Above all, he is concerned with ethical behavior. How believers act, he says, has eschatological significance—future reward or punishment depends on it. In this regard, James bemoans the inconsistency of human behavior (1:6–8,22–24; 2:14–17; 4:1,2). Human beings are "double-minded" (1:8; 4:8), in sharp contrast to God, who is one (2:19).

James has been incorrectly understood by some to contradict Paul's doctrine of justification by faith (2:14–26). If James had Paul in mind at all, he was addressing himself to those who had perverted Paul's message, insisting that it doesn't matter what you do, as long as you have faith. James responded by asserting that works are the outward evidence of inner faith. Works make faith visible to others. In contrast, Paul was concerned with our standing before God. As is evident from Romans 12–15, Paul certainly agreed with James that faith in Christ has direct implications for how believers live.

Ice-Breaker — 15 Min.

Be sure to read the introductory material in the front of this book prior to the first session. To help your group members get acquainted, introduce each person and then take turns answering one or two of the Ice-Breaker questions.

Testing can be looked on as a burdensome trial or an invigorating challenge. Take turns sharing with one another from your own experiences with ordinary tests.

1. In high school or college, how much studying did you do before an exam?

   ○ Crammed the night before.
   ○ Studied diligently for two weeks beforehand.
   ○ Just "winged"it because I forgot all about the test until the last minute.
   ○ Memorized all four hundred pages of notes verbatim.
   ○ Other _____.

2. How many times did you have to take your driver's test before you got your first license?

3. What is your attitude towards taking tests?

   ○ I enjoy the challenge.
   ○ I hate the stress.
   ○ I don't hate tests, but I am glad to be out of school.
   ○ I still have nightmares about long horrible exams.

Bible Study — 30 Min.

READ SCRIPTURE AND DISCUSS

Ask a member of the group, selected ahead of time, to read the passage aloud. Then discuss the Questions for Interaction, dividing into subgroups of three to six as necessary. Be sure to save at least 15 minutes for the Caring Time.

Most of us don't welcome trials into our lives or enjoy suffering, but James shows us a different way of looking at things. He also gives some important instructions regarding wisdom and the proper attitude towards material prosperity. Read James 1:1–11, and consider the purpose testing serves in our lives.

Consider it Joy

1 James, a slave of God and of the Lord Jesus Christ:
To the twelve tribes in the Dispersion.
Greetings.
²Consider it a great joy, my brothers, whenever you experience various trials, ³knowing that the testing of your faith produces endurance. ⁴But endurance must do its complete work, so that you may be mature and complete, lacking nothing.

⁵Now if any of you lacks wisdom, he should ask God, who gives to all generously and without criticizing, and it will be given to him. ⁶But let him ask in faith without doubting. For the doubter is like the surging sea, driven and tossed by the wind. ⁷That person should not expect to receive anything from the Lord. ⁸An indecisive man is unstable in all his ways.

⁹The brother of humble circumstances should boast in his exaltation; ¹⁰but the one who is rich should boast in his humiliation, because he will pass away like a flower of the field. ¹¹For the sun rises with its scorching heat and dries up the grass; its flower falls off, and its beautiful appearance is destroyed. In the same way, the rich man will wither away while pursuing his activities.

James 1:1–11

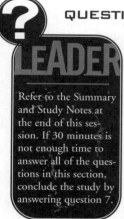

QUESTIONS FOR INTERACTION

Refer to the Summary and Study Notes at the end of this session. If 30 minutes is not enough time to answer all of the questions in this section, conclude the study by answering question 7.

1. What task or project have you accomplished that required great perseverance?

2. According to James, what should a Christian's attitude be when facing trials? How often is this your attitude in your own hard times?

3. Why is enduring important? What reward comes with enduring in the faith?

4. What does it mean to be "mature and complete" (v. 4)? Who do you know that you think could be described this way? What characteristics do you see in this person's life?

5. How does James turn the assumed status of rich and poor upside down? How does this affect the way you think about your own financial position?

   ○ It makes me nervous, what if God should humble me because of my wealth.
   ○ I feel pretty good, because I never really had anything.
   ○ I feel like I have been wasting my life.
   ○ Maybe I really am fairly well off.
   ○ I want to understand how God really values wealth.
   ○ Other _____.

6. What is a trial you have faced in your life? What helped you through it?

7. In what area of your life do you need wisdom from God right now? What has kept you from asking for it?

GOING DEEPER:

If your group has time and/or wants a challenge, go on to this question.

8. Verse 7 tells us that a doubter need not expect to receive anything from the Lord. How does this fit with verse 5 which says that God "gives to all generously and without criticizing?" If you ever experience doubts about your faith, does that necessarily mean that you are "unstable in all your ways?"

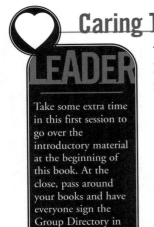

Caring Time   15 Min.

APPLY THE LESSON AND PRAY FOR ONE ANOTHER

It is very important for group development to express your concern for each other by praying for one another.

Take some extra time in this first session to go over the introductory material at the beginning of this book. At the close, pass around your books and have everyone sign the Group Directory in the front.

1. Agree on the group covenant and ground rules which are described in the introduction to this book.

2. Begin the prayer time by taking turns and completing the following sentence: "The biggest test to my faith right now is ... "

3. Share any other prayer requests and then close in prayer. Pray specifically for God to lead you to someone to bring next week to fill the empty chair.

Next Week

Today we began our study of the book of James by discussing what trials and struggles are good for, and how we should respond to them in our own lives. We also talked about God as the source of wisdom and were encouraged to realize that he will give us the wisdom we need to deal with our lives—we only have to ask him for it. During the coming week, be sure to ask God for the wisdom you need. Thank him for his willingness to give it to you, and ask him to help you keep a joyful attitude toward your trials. Next week we will continue to talk about the blessings that come from enduring trials to the glory of God.

SUMMARY: James begins his letter in the same way most Greek letters began—by naming the sender and the recipient and then by offering a greeting. The letter is primarily concerned with practical instructions for Christian living. This section introduces three themes: trials and testing, wisdom from God, and proper attitudes toward wealth.

1:1 James. This probably refers to the brother of Jesus who was known in the early church as "James the Just." Extra-biblical accounts tell us that James was martyred in A.D. 62. The high priest Annas the Younger seized James, who was then condemned and stoned to death. A few years later, in A.D. 66, the church in Jerusalem (which James headed) came to an end. Fearing the approaching Roman armies, the church members fled to Pella in the Transjordan and never returned to Jerusalem. **a slave.** James is so well-known that he needs no further designation. In fact, in the letter of Jude this wide recognition of James is used by the author to identify himself: "Jude, a servant of Jesus Christ and a brother of James." (In contrast, it is often necessary for Paul to identify himself as an apostle, thereby asserting his apostolic authority in the matters about which he is writing.) James' modest designation of himself as "a slave" instead of "Bishop of Jerusalem" or "the brother of Jesus" is probably a reflection of his genuine humility. Here he identifies Jesus as the "Lord" (master), therefore the appropriate relationship of all others to Jesus is as servants (literally "slaves"). **the twelve tribes.** This is a term used in the Old Testament to refer to the nation of Israel, even after 10 of the 12 tribes were lost and never reconstituted following Israel's captivity by the Assyrians. In the New Testament, it came to be associated with the Christian church. Gentile Christians saw themselves as joint heirs with Israel (Rom. 4; 9:24–26; Phil. 3:3; 1 Peter 2:9–10). **Dispersion.** The word is literally *diaspora* and was used by Jews to refer to those of their number living outside Palestine in the Gentile world. Here it probably refers to those Jewish Christians living outside Palestine (1 Peter 1:1).

1:2–11 The three themes (testing, wisdom and riches) are connected. In order to survive the test regarding how one treats riches, wisdom from God is needed. James uses verbal echoes to link together this section. 1:1 is linked to 1:2 by the similar sound of *chairein* (greetings) and *charan* (joy). 1:2–4 are connected by the repeated word "perseverance." Then 1:2–4 is linked to 1:5–8 by the word "lack." The word "ask" is repeated in verses 5 and 6. The word "pride" links verses 9 and 10.

1:2 Consider it a great joy. Christians ought to view the difficulties of life with enthusiasm, because the outcome of trials will be beneficial. The joy James is talking about is not just a feeling, however. It is an active acceptance of adversity. **my brothers.** James is addressing his letter to those who are members of the church. This is not a letter for the world at large. The phrase "my brothers" carries with it a sense of warmth. Even though in the course of his letter James will say some very harsh things to these brothers and sisters, it is never with the sense that they are despised or even different from him (3:1–2). This is family. "My brothers" is a recurrent phrase in James, often used when a new subject is introduced (1:2,19; 2:14; 3:1; 5:7). **various trials.** The word "trials" has the dual sense of "adversity" (disease, persecution, tragedy) and "temptations" (lust, greed, trust in wealth). James is not urging Christians to seek trials. Trials will come on their own. This is simply the way life is; especially it seems, for a first-century Christian whose church is being persecuted.

1:3 One reason that the Christian can rejoice in suffering is that immediate good does come out of the pain. In this verse James assumes that there will be good results. **endurance.** Or "perseverance." It is used in the sense of active overcoming, rather than passive acceptance. This is a virtue vital to the Christian life, coming mainly out of trials, it seems.

1:4 *its complete work.* Perfection is not automatic—it takes time and effort. *mature and complete.* What James has in mind here is wholeness of character. He is not calling for some sort of esoteric perfection or sinlessness. Instead, the emphasis is on moral blamelessness. He is thinking of the integrated life, in contrast to the divided person of verses 6–8. To be mature is to have reached a certain stage or to have fulfilled a given purpose. An animal had to be fully developed to be fit for sacrifice to God. To be complete is to have no flaws or blemishes. *lacking.* The opposite of mature and complete. This is a word used of an army that has been defeated or a person who has failed to reach a certain standard.

1:5 *wisdom.* This is not just abstract knowledge, but God-given insight which leads to right living. It is the ability to make right decisions, especially about moral issues (as one must do during trials). *generously.* A reference both to the abundance of the gift and the spirit with which it is given. God gives fully, without hesitation and without grudging (2 Cor. 8:1–2).

1:6 James now contrasts the readiness on God's part to give (v. 5) with the hesitation on people's part to ask (v. 6). Both here and in 4:3, unanswered prayer is connected to the quality of the asking, not to the unwillingness of God to give. *ask in faith.* To be in one mind about God's ability to answer prayer, to be sure that God will hear and will act in accord with his superior wisdom. The ability to pray this sort of trusting prayer is an example of the character which is produced by trials.

1:8 *indecisive.* To doubt is to be in two minds—to believe and to disbelieve simultaneously; to be torn between two impulses—one positive, one negative.

1:9–11 Poverty is an example of a trial to be endured—but so too are riches, though in quite a different way. The question of riches and poverty is the third major theme in the book.

1:9 *humble circumstances.* Those who are poor in a material and social sense, and who are looked down on by others because they are poor. *boast.* Such boasting is equivalent to the rejoicing that is encouraged in verse 2 in the face of adversity. This becomes possible when the poor see beyond immediate circumstances to their new position as children of God. They may be poor in worldly goods, but they are rich beyond imagination since they are children of God and thus heirs of the whole world. Therefore, they do in fact have a superior position in life and ought to rejoice in it. *exaltation.* In the early church, the poor gained a new sense of self-respect. Slaves found that traditional social distinctions had been obliterated (Gal. 3:28).

1:10 *rich.* The peril of riches is that people come to trust in wealth as a source of security. It is a mark of double-mindedness to attempt to serve both God and money. *humiliation.* Jewish culture understood wealth to be a sure sign of God's favor. Here, as elsewhere (vv. 2,9), James reverses conventional expectations. *flower of the field.* In February, Spring comes to Palestine with a blaze of color, as flowers like the lily, the poppy, and the lupine blossom along with a carpet of grass. By May, however, all the flowers and grass are brown.

1:11 *scorching heat.* The hot, southeast desert wind (the sirocco) sweeps into Palestine in the Spring like a blast of hot air. It blows day and night until the verdant cover is withered and brown. *its flower falls off.* Wealth gives an uncertain security, since it is apt to be swept away as abruptly as desert flowers (Isa. 40:6–8).

SeSSIoN 2
Trials and Temptations
SCRIPTURE JAMES 1:12–18

Last Week

In last week's lesson we began the discussion of how the believer should deal with trials and testings, and we discussed James' instructions about having an attitude of joy in the midst of our troubles. Today we will continue this theme as we talk about where temptations come from in our lives.

Ice-Breaker   15 Min.

CONNECT WITH YOUR GROUP

Begin the session with a word of prayer. Have your group members take turns sharing their responses to one, two or all three of the Ice-Breaker questions. Be sure that everyone gets a chance to participate

Some things in our lives require enduring some kind of struggle or discomfort in order to get what we want. Tell one another about your own experiences with persevering to gain an end.

1. Looking back on your childhood, what skill was particularly difficult to master? Did you have someone to help you achieve your goals?

2. When you were in high school did you go out for sports or music? Did you ever receive any recognition for your hard work?

3. Of all the goals you have worked to reach, which one has given you the most satisfaction? Which one gives the least?

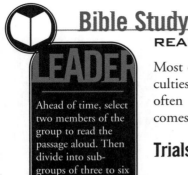

Bible Study   30 Min.

READ SCRIPTURE AND DISCUSS

Ahead of time, select two members of the group to read the passage aloud. Then divide into sub-groups of three to six to discuss the Questions for Interaction.

Most of us would like to think that all our temptations and diffi-culties come from outside sources, but actually the reverse is most often true. Read James 1:12–18 and discover where temptation comes from, and also where all good things come from.

Trials and Temptations

Reader One: ¹²Blessed is a man who endures trials,

Reader Two: because when he passes the test he will receive the crown of life that He has promised to those who love Him. ¹³No one undergoing a trial should say,

Reader One: "I am being tempted by God."

Reader Two: For God is not tempted by evil, and He Himself doesn't tempt anyone. ¹⁴But each per-son is tempted when he is drawn away and enticed by his own evil desires. ¹⁵Then after desire has conceived, it gives birth to sin, and when sin is fully grown, it gives birth to death.

Reader One: ¹⁶Don't be deceived, my dearly loved brothers. ¹⁷Every generous act and every perfect gift is from above, coming down from the Father of lights; with Him there is no vari-ation or shadow cast by turning. ¹⁸By His own choice, He gave us a new birth by the message of truth so that we would be the firstfruits of His creatures.

James 1:12–18

QUESTIONS FOR INTERACTION

Refer to the Summary and Study Notes at the end of this session as needed. If 30 min-utes is not enough time to answer all of the questions in this section, conclude the Bible Study by answering question 7.

1. Who do you know who deserves a special award for enduring tri-als?

2. What is the "crown of life" offered to those who endure?

   ○ A crown passed down by the Apostles from generation to generation.
   ○ A laurel like that given to an ancient athlete.
   ○ A halo like an angel would wear.
   ○ A special blessing resulting from good works.
   ○ Eternal life.
   ○ The ability to fully enjoy heaven.
   ○ Reward for enduring trials.
   ○ Other _____.

   What seems to be the conditions attached to receiving this crown?

3. What do we learn in this passage about the origin of temptation? How does this affect the way that you look at your struggles and problems?

4. What stages does temptation pass through to become full-blown sin? How can you see that this has happened in your own life?

5. If "every generous act and every perfect gift" (v. 17) comes from God, what does this say about "good people" who reject God because they think they do not need him?

6. What encouragement do you find in verses 17 and 18?

7. What have you found to be most helpful in dealing with temptation? What specific temptations or trials are you facing right now that you need strength to endure?

GOING DEEPER:

If your group has time and/or wants a challenge, go on to this question.

8. What is the connection between "passing the test" and receiving the "crown of life" (v. 12)? Is this passage saying that receiving the crown is dependent upon our own actions (because the test is passed and the crown is received), or is it merely a statement about the chronology (first the test and then the crown)? Does one have to undergo testing in order to receive the crown?

Caring Time   15 Min.

APPLY THE LESSON AND PRAY FOR ONE ANOTHER

Take time now to encourage and strengthen one another to endure the trials and temptations in your lives. Listen as each one shares responses to the following questions and then pray together for the needs mentioned.

LEADER

Bring the group members back together for the Caring Time. Begin by sharing responses to all three questions. Then share prayer requests and close in a group prayer. Those who do not feel comfortable praying out loud should not feel pressured to do so. As the leader, conclude the prayer time and be sure to pray for the empty chair.

1. What good gift have you received from God (v. 17) for which you are thankful?

2. How can this group pray for the needs you mentioned in question 7?

3. Share any other requests or praises that you would like to bring before the Lord right now.

Next Week

Today we discussed the important topic of dealing with temptations. We realized that our own sinful nature is responsible for the evil we do, but we were also encouraged by the fact that God, who does not change, has chosen us to be born again. During the coming week, ask God to make you aware of your own evil desires and to help you to stop them before they give birth to sin. Next week our session focuses on the relationship between hearing the word and taking action on what we hear.

Notes on James 1:12–18

SUMMARY: James now launches into the second statement of his three themes. Here the subject is trials and he expands on what he said about trials in verses 2–4. Here he adds two more pieces of information. In verse 12 he tells us that trials bring blessedness because out of them one receives the crown of life. In verses 2–4 the emphasis was on the joy of testing because it brings maturity. Then in verses 13–15 he looks at the source of failure during a trial. It is not God who is causing one to fail. Rather, it is one's own evil desires.

1:12 *Blessed.* Happy is the person who has withstood all the trials to the end. *endures.* In verse 3, James says that testing produces perseverance. Here he points out that such perseverance brings the reward of blessedness. *passes the test.* Such a person is like metal which has been refined by fire and is purified of all foreign substances. *crown of life.* As with Paul (Rom. 5:1–5) and Peter (1 Peter 1:6–7), James now focuses on the final result of endurance under trial: eternal life. Crowns were worn at weddings and feasts and so signify joy. They were given to the winner of an athletic competition and so signify victory. Finally, they were worn by royalty as befits children of God the King.

1:13–15 Perseverance under trial is not the only option. People can fail. In these verses James examines the causes of such failure.

1:13 The focus shifts from enduring outward trials (v. 12) to resisting inner temptations. Verse 12 is linked to verse 13 by a verbal echo: *peirasmos* (trial) in verse 12 and *perirazo* (temptation) in verse 13. *"I am being tempted by God."* The natural tendency is to blame others for our failure. In

this case, God is blamed for sending a test that was too hard to bear. The first-century Jewish Christians might reason in this fashion as a consequence of rabbinic teaching. Noting that human beings are double-minded and so inclined toward both good and evil, some rabbis concluded in the same way that if God was responsible for the positive side of human nature, he was also responsible for the evil side. One rabbinic saying reads: "God said, 'It repents me that I created the evil tendency in man ... !'" James stands opposed to this view. God does not put people into situations in order to test them. Such temptations arise quite naturally from life itself. James will go on to say in verse 14 that what turns a natural situation into a temptation is evil desire within a person. *God is not tempted by evil, and He himself doesn't tempt anyone.* God does not lure anyone into a tempting situation just to see whether that person will stand or fall. That is not God's nature. He neither desires evil nor causes evil.

1:14–15 The steps in temptation are explained by reference to the birth process ("conceived," "birth," "fully grown"). The possibility of an evil act is entertained, then acted on again and again as the thought becomes a deed and until it finally brings death. In fact, the picture here is of a seductress who entices a victim into her bed and conceives a child whose name is sin. This child, in turn, produces his own offspring which is the monster called death. This same chain from desire to sin to death is described by Paul in Romans 7:7–12.

1:14 *drawn away and enticed.* We are tricked by our own sinful natures in the same way that a fish is tricked by the lure, only to discover too late that there is a painful hook beneath the entrancing exterior. *evil desires.* The true source of evil is a person's own inner inclination (Mark 7:21–23).

1:15 *death.* The opposite of "the crown of life"; the point of no-return where a repeated act has become so ingrained that we have no ability to restrain ourselves.

1:16–18 God doesn't send the test; he sends the gift of wisdom to help us meet the trial. Far from tempting people, God gives gifts, most notably the gift of new life.

1:17 This is a line of Greek poetry, either original or a quotation from an unknown source. *Father of lights.* God is the creator of the stars. *shadow cast by turning.* All created things, even stars, change and vary. God does not.

1:18 *birth.* The contrast is made between sin which gives birth to death and the Gospel (the word of truth), which gives birth to life and brings into being God's children. *firstfruits.* At the beginning of the harvest, the earliest produce was offered to God as a symbol that the whole harvest was his.

SeSSIoN 3
Listening and Doing
SCRIPTURE JAMES 1:19–27

Last Week

Last week's session dealt with the subject of temptations. We talked about the rewards of enduring trials, and the origin of our struggles with sin. We were also encouraged by the realization that God has chosen us to be re-born through the Gospel. Today our study will focus on the relationship between hearing God's Word, and putting it into practice in our lives.

Ice-Breaker   15 Min.

CONNECT WITH YOUR GROUP

LEADER

Choose one or two of the Ice-Breaker questions. If you have a new group member you may want to do all three. Remember to stick closely to the three-part agenda and the time allowed for each segment.

Everyone likes to be heard, but we are not always good at listening to others. Enjoy getting to know one another better as you take turns answering the following questions.

1. Who in your life has been a good "listening ear" when you needed one?

2. When you were a child, did you ever pretend that you didn't hear when your mother or father told you to do something?

3. Would you describe yourself as a talker or the more quiet type? How do you think your friends would describe you?

READ SCRIPTURE AND DISCUSS

LEADER

Have two members of the group, selected ahead of time, read aloud the Scripture passage. Then discuss the Questions for Interaction, dividing into subgroups of three to six.

This passage deals with the important issue of making sure that we don't just hear God's Word, say "yeah, yeah," and move on in our lives. We must actually apply it to our daily lives. Read James 1:19–27 and take special note of the specific practical instructions that James gives for keeping our lives in line with God's way.

Listening and Doing

Reader One: ¹⁹My dearly loved brothers, understand this: everyone must be quick to hear, slow to speak, and slow to anger, ²⁰for man's anger does not accomplish God's righteousness. ²¹Therefore, ridding yourselves of all moral filth and evil excess, humbly receive the implanted word, which is able to save you.

Reader Two: ²²But be doers of the word and not hearers only, deceiving yourselves. ²³Because if anyone is a hearer of the word and not a doer, he is like a man looking at his own face in a mirror; ²⁴for he looks at himself, goes away, and right away forgets what kind of man he was.

Reader One: ²⁵But the one who looks intently into the perfect law of freedom and perseveres in it, and is not a forgetful hearer but a doer who acts—this person will be blessed in what he does.

Reader Two: ²⁶If anyone thinks he is religious, without controlling his tongue but deceiving his heart, his religion is useless.

Reader One: ²⁷Pure and undefiled religion before our God and Father is this:

Reader Two: to look after orphans and widows in their distress and to keep oneself unstained by the world.

James 1:19–27

QUESTIONS FOR INTERACTION

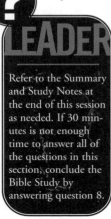

LEADER

Refer to the Summary and Study Notes at the end of this session as needed. If 30 minutes is not enough time to answer all of the questions in this section, conclude the Bible Study by answering question 8.

1. When it comes to getting angry, do you tend to have a long or a short fuse? When was a time you wish you had been "quick to hear" and "slow to speak" (v. 19)?

2. Do you know someone whom you would categorize as a "doer"? What stands out about this person's life?

3. Of the three areas mentioned in verse 19, mark on the line where you would you rate yourself?

Hearing: quick _____ slow
Speaking: quick _____ slow
Anger: quick _____ slow
Which needs the most improvement? How can you apply verse 26 to your own life?

4. What is the "implanted word" and how is it able to save you?

5. What qualifies as "moral filth" and "evil excess?" How can you get rid of these, or avoid them?

6. What is the "perfect law of freedom"? How could law and freedom go together?

7. What does it mean to "keep oneself unstained by the world" (v.27)?

○ Become a hermit in a haircloth shirt in order to avoid all contact with unbelievers.
○ Try to use discretion in entertainment choices.
○ Show by your lifestyle that you march to a different drummer.
○ Be friendly to your neighbors, but only spend time with other believers.
○ Mix freely with unbelievers, but keep a personal standard that is different from the world.
○ Other _____.

8. In what area of your life could you do a better job of applying God's Word rather than merely listening to it? What can you do to change this?

GOING DEEPER:

If your group has time and/or wants a challenge, go on to this question.

9. Verse 20 says that "man's anger does not accomplish God's righteousness." Does anger ever accomplish good? Is there room for "righteous wrath" in the Christian life, such as when Jesus drove the moneychangers out of the temple? How can we know the difference between man's anger and righteous wrath?

Caring Time

APPLY THE LESSON AND PRAY FOR ONE ANOTHER

Part of growing as a Christian includes reaching out to others. Use this time together to encourage one another and to pray for the needs of each member of the group.

LEADER

Begin the Caring Time by having group members take turns sharing responses to all three questions. Be sure to save at least the last five minutes for a time of group prayer.

1. What is something this group can plan to do together to demonstrate "pure undefiled religion?"

2. How can this group pray for you as you seek to become a "doer" in the area you mentioned in question 8?

3. How can this group be a listening ear for you right now?

Next Week

Today we discussed a passage that is packed with practical instructions for Christian living. It particularly focused on how important it is not just to hear God's Word, but to really put it into practice. During the coming week, review these verses and see what you can do to put into practice the Word of God. Is there a needy person you can help? How can you be a better listener to your spouse or child? Do you need to work on controlling your temper? Ask God to help you to become a "doer of the word." Next week we will discuss how Christians should treat each other without favoritism.

Notes on James 1:19–27

SUMMARY: In chapter one James twice introduces the three main subjects of his book. In this passage he identifies for the second time, the second and third points he will discuss in his book—speech (vv. 19–21) and generosity (vv. 22–27). Having just mentioned God's Word (v. 18), James shifts here to the subject of human words. From the "word of truth" he moves to the "word of anger." James is still, in fact, focusing on the theme of wisdom, except that now his concern is with the relationship between wisdom and speech—a connection he will make plainer in 3:1–4:12.

1:19 *quick to hear.* The heart of what James wants to say is found in this proverb. This is not a new teaching. The Bible often commends the value of listening and the danger of hasty speech (3:1–12; Prov. 10:19; 13:3; 17:28; 29:20; Matt. 12:36–37). *slow to speak.* One needs to consider carefully what is to be said, rather than impulsively and carelessly launching into words that are not wise. *slow to anger.* James does not forbid anger. Repressed anger will eventually come out and then it can be quite destructive. Also, at times, anger is the only appropriate response to a situation. James' point is that anger should not be the stock answer to all our problems. Anger must be saved for those times when it is just.

1:20 This verse is reminiscent of what Jesus said in the Sermon on the Mount (Matt. 5:21–22). Human anger does not produce the kind of life that God wants.

1:21 If Christians are to speak wisely, they must prepare to do so by the dual action of ridding themselves of all that is corrupt and not godly, and then by humbly relying upon the Word of God which is within them already. *ridding yourselves.* This verb means literally, "to lay aside" or "to strip off," as one would do with filthy clothing. To be in tune with God's purpose first requires this negative action—this rejection or repentance of all that drags one down. *all moral filth.* The two Greek words here refer to actual dirt and are used as a metaphor for moral uncleanness. *evil excess.* The Revised Standard Version translates it as "rank growth of wickedness." NIV uses the expression "evil that is so prevalent." *humbly receive.* Having renounced evil (a negative act), the next step is to accept that which is good (a

positive act). This same twofold action of repentance and faith—rejecting evil and accepting God—is the path whereby people come to Christian faith in the first place. Repentance and faith are also the key to living out the Christian life. James has already twice mentioned the idea of receiving God's gifts (vv. 5 and 17). This receiving must be done humbly. This attitude contrasts directly with the anger about which he just spoke. *implanted word.* They are Christians already. They have the life of God in them. It is now up to them to act upon what is already theirs. They must actualize in their lives the truth of God. This is the same "word of truth" mentioned in verse 18. In contrast to the quick and angry words of people—words which hurt and destroy—there is the Word of God which saves.

1:22–27 James begins by talking about accepting the Word of God (v. 21) and then moves on to the concept of internalizing and acting upon this Word. Thus he moves from proper speech to proper action, which in this case is charity toward those in need. In this way he gets to his third theme, the idea that Christians are called upon to be generous in the face of poverty.

1:22 *be doers of the word.* This is James' main point in this section. *hearers only.* The Christian must not just hear the Word of God. A response is required. *deceiving yourselves.* It does not matter how well a person may know the teaching of the apostles or how much Scripture he or she has memorized. To make mere knowledge of God's will the sole criterion for the religious life is dangerous and self-deceptive.

1:23–24 James illustrates his point with a metaphor. Scripture is a mirror to the Christian, because in it his or her true state is shown. The person who reads it and then goes away unchanged is like the person who gets up in the morning and sees how dirty and disheveled he is, but then promptly forgets about it. The proper response would be to get cleaned up.

1:25 In contrast is the person who acts to correct what is discovered to be wrong and continues acting in this way. *the perfect law.* The reference is probably to the teachings of Jesus which set one free, in distinction to the Jewish Law which brought bondage (Rom. 8:2). *perseveres.* Such people do not merely notice a command and then act on it once, but they make that insight a continuing part of their lives. *blessed.* The sheer act of keeping this law is a happy experience in and of itself because it produces good fruit, now and in the future.

1:26–27 In these verses, James sums up what he has said in chapter 1 by way of introduction. He says that the mark of the true Christian is first, the ability to control the tongue (the theme of speech and wisdom); second, the willingness to engage in acts of charity (the theme of generosity); and third, the attempt to overcome the trials and temptations offered by the world (the theme of testing).

1:26 *If anyone thinks.* The focus is on a person's own self-assessment of his or her religious commitment. In contrast, in verse 27, James states what God considers as truly religious. *religious.* The emphasis here is probably on the overt acts of religion, such as scrupulous observance of the details of worship and personal acts of piety. *controlling his tongue.* The inability to control one's speech (as in gossip and criticism) is the mark of the person who thinks he or she is religious but really is not.

1:27 *religion.* True religion, it turns out, has more to do with acts of charity than acts of piety. It involves caring for others and avoiding the corrupting influence of one's culture. *orphans and widows.* In the Old Testament, orphans and widows are the poor and oppressed, whom God's people are to care for because God cares for them (Deut. 10:17–18; 24:17–22). A child without the protection and provision of parents is at the mercy of the community. So too is the widow who typically had an insecure place in ancient society. A widow also found it difficult to support herself given the social situation of the times. *unstained.* Unpolluted, pure, undefiled. *world.* This refers to the world system that is in opposition to God.

SeSSIoN 4
Favoritism Forbidden
SCRIPTURE JAMES 2:1–13

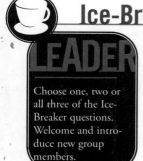

Last Week

In the session last week, we talked about the importance of being a doer of the word and not a hearer only. We talked about some specific ways that we can do this in our daily lives. This week's session focuses on how we as Christians should treat one another.

Ice-Breaker   15 Min.

CONNECT WITH YOUR GROUP

LEADER

Choose one, two or all three of the Ice-Breaker questions. Welcome and introduce new group members.

Enjoy getting to know one another as you take turns answering the following questions about best seats and fine clothes.

1. What is your favorite outfit to wear?

  ○ Full evening dress—because I feel so elegant.
  ○ Full sweats—because they are so comfortable.
  ○ Dressy casuals—because I fit in anywhere.
  ○ Tees and shorts—it is just me.
  ○ Other _____.

2. For what event would you buy the best seats in the house?

  ○ The Super Bowl.
  ○ A Broadway play.
  ○ A concert by your favorite group.
  ○ The local symphony playing music from a composer you like.
  ○ Other _____.

3. When have you shown up at a gathering over- or under-dressed? How did you feel?

Bible Study

READ SCRIPTURE AND DISCUSS

LEADER

Select a member of the group ahead of time to read the passage aloud. Then divide into smaller groups to discuss the Questions for Interaction.

In our casual society it might seem that discussions about fine clothing and most-honored seats don't really apply, but if we look more closely we will find that we are affected more than we think. Read James 2:1-13 and see what God's Word has to say about showing favoritism.

Favoritism Forbidden

2 My brothers, hold your faith in our glorious Lord Jesus Christ without showing favoritism. ²For suppose a man comes into your meeting wearing a gold ring, dressed in fine clothes, and a poor man dressed in dirty clothes also comes in. ³If you look with favor on the man wearing the fine clothes so that you say, "Sit here in a good place," and yet you say to the poor man, "Stand over there," or, "Sit here on the floor by my footstool," ⁴haven't you discriminated among yourselves and become judges with evil thoughts?

⁵Listen, my dear brothers: Didn't God choose the poor in this world to be rich in faith and heirs of the kingdom that He has promised to those who love Him? ⁶Yet you dishonored that poor man. Don't the rich oppress you and drag you into the courts? ⁷Don't they blaspheme the noble name that you bear?

⁸If you really carry out the royal law prescribed in Scripture, "You shall love your neighbor as yourself," you are doing well. ⁹But if you show favoritism, you commit sin and are convicted by the law as transgressors. ¹⁰For whoever keeps the entire law, yet fails in one point, is guilty of breaking it all. ¹¹For He who said, "Do not commit adultery," also said, "Do not murder." So if you do not commit adultery, but you do murder, you are a lawbreaker.

¹²Speak and act as those who will be judged by the law of freedom. ¹³For judgment is without mercy to the one who hasn't shown mercy. Mercy triumphs over judgment.

James 2:1–13

QUESTIONS FOR INTERACTION

LEADER

Refer to the Summary and Study Notes at the end of this session as needed. If 30 minutes is not enough time to answer all of the questions in this section, conclude the Bible Study by answering question 7.

1. In general, what do you think are some ways that people show favoritism in our society today? Of the ways listed below which one is the most problematic?

- ○ Giving honor to athletes.
- ○ Not noticing servers or custodians.
- ○ Showing favor to the rich and famous.
- ○ Treating people different because of family heritage.
- ○ Socializing only with those who are similar.
- ○ Noticing the beautiful people over the common.
- ○ Other _____.

2. In what ways might you have been guilty of showing favoritism? What do you think the results have been? When has someone shown favoritism to you? Or to someone else at your expense?

3. Of all the people in your life, who would you describe as being the "richest in faith?" What stands out about this person's life?

4. In verses 5–7 James clearly links poverty with riches in faith and material wealth with oppression. How could being poor affect your spiritual life? How could money hinder being rich in faith?

5. What is the point James is making about the Law in verses 8–11?

6. Do you feel that you are better at showing mercy or receiving it? When has someone shown mercy to you?

7. What do you think needs to be changed in your life so that you will be following the "royal law?" What is one practical way that you can "love your neighbor as yourself" this week?

GOING DEEPER:

If your group has time and/or wants a challenge, go on to this question.

8. What is the relationship between mercy and judgment? Is verse 13 saying that God will not forgive us if we have not forgiven? What is the law of freedom by which we will be judged?

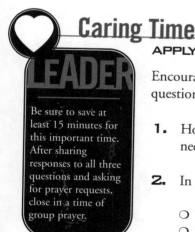

Caring Time   15 Min.

APPLY THE LESSON AND PRAY FOR ONE ANOTHER

Be sure to save at least 15 minutes for this important time. After sharing responses to all three questions and asking for prayer requests, close in a time of group prayer.

Encourage one another in your faith by discussing the following questions and sharing prayer requests.

1. How "rich in faith" have you been feeling lately? What do you need to rejuvenate your spiritual life?

2. In your life right now, who do you identify with the most?

  ○ The poor man in dirty clothes.
  ○ The rich man in fine clothes.
  ○ The one who is catering to the rich.
  ○ Other _____.

3. How can this group do a better job of supporting and encouraging one another?

Next Week

Today our lesson focused on the important topic of how Christians should treat each other. James specifically discussed the problem of judging a person's character by how the person is dressed. We were reminded of Christ's "royal law" that is supposed to govern all of our relationships. This week, put into practice your answer to question 7 above and work on treating every person with whom you have contact in the way you like to be treated. Next week we will continue the discussion of proper Christian behavior as we talk about the relationship between faith and works.

Notes on James 2:1–13

SUMMARY: James now begins his exposition of his first theme: poverty and generosity (2:1–26). Notice that he treats these themes in the reverse order from the way in which he presented them in his introduction. In this chapter his focus is on the question of the rich and the poor. Christians are to have a different ethic than that of the world. They are not to favor the wealthy simply because they are wealthy, nor are they to despise the poor simply because they are poor. The poor are to be welcomed and aided. In fact, one's faith is shown by acts of generosity to the poor. The first half of the chapter (2:1–13) focuses on a warning against prejudice.

2:1–9 James' point is quite straightforward: to discriminate between people is inconsistent with the Christian faith. This is another example of how Christian faith must be expressed in right behavior.

2:1 James appeals to them as believers in "our glorious Lord Jesus Christ" not to discriminate. His reason is that Jesus alone is the "glorious Lord." There is only one Lord and he saves both rich and poor on the same basis—belief in him. Rich and poor are alike before their common Lord. *glorious.* Jesus is described here by means of a word that denotes the presence of God. When God draws near, what people experience is the light of his splendor (Ex. 16:10; 2 Chron. 7:1–3; Ezek. 8:4; Mark 9:2–7; Luke 2:9). James' point is that in Jesus one sees a manifestation of God's presence. *favoritism.* This is the act of paying special attention to someone because he or she is rich, important, famous, powerful, etc. Such discrimination (respect of persons) is condemned throughout Scripture (Mal. 2:9; Acts 10:34–45; Rom. 2:11; Eph. 6:9; Col. 3:25).

2:2–4 James now gives a specific example of how deference to the rich operates in the church. The situation he describes could well have happened in the first-century church, as it was one of the few institutions where traditional social barriers had been dropped. It would have been quite possible for a wealthy landowner to belong to the same Christian assembly as one of his slaves.

2:2 *meeting.* The word translated "meeting" is literally "synagogue." *a gold ring.* This is the mark of those who belonged to the equestrian order—the second level of Roman aristocracy. These noblemen were typically wealthy. Rings in general were a sign of wealth. The more ostentatious would fill their fingers with rings. Early Christians were urged to wear only one ring, on the little finger, bearing the image of a dove, fish, or anchor. *fine clothes.* These are literally "bright and shining" garments, like those worn by the angels in Acts 10:30. *poor man.* The word used here denotes a beggar, a person from the lowest level of society. Had this been a low-paid worker, a different

Greek word would probably have been used. *dirty clothes.* In contrast to the spotless garments of the rich man, the beggar wears filthy rags, probably because this is all he owns.

2:4 James condemns this behavior on two grounds. First, they are making distinctions between people when, in fact, Christ came to remove all such barriers (Gal. 3:28). Second, they are prejudicing their judicial decision in favor of the rich person and not listening only to the merits of the case.

2:4–7 James attacks this kind of discrimination. All social distinctions are null and void in the church. Partiality is clearly out of place. Both rich and poor are to be received equally. Notice that the rich are not condemned here. They are welcome in the church. What is condemned is the insult to the poor person (v. 6).

2:5 *the poor.* The New Testament is clearly on the side of the poor. In Jesus' first sermon he declared that he was called to preach the Gospel to the poor (Luke 4:18). When John the Baptist questioned whether Jesus was actually the Messiah, in response Jesus pointed to his preaching to the poor (Matt. 11:4–5). The poor are called blessed (Luke 6:20). The poor flocked to Jesus during his ministry and later into his church (1 Cor. 1:26).

2:6 *Yet you dishonored that poor man.* The Old Testament also condemns this behavior (Prov. 14:21). *oppress you.* In a day of abject poverty the poor were often forced to borrow money at exorbitant rates of interest just to survive. The rich profited from their need. *drag you into the courts.* This was probably over the issue of a debt.

2:7 James levels a third charge at the rich. Not only do they exploit the poor and harass them in court, they also mock the name of Jesus. This could be expected since the church was largely a collection of poor people and thus would be the object of scorn by the wealthy. *the noble name.* The early followers of Jesus were dubbed with the name "Christians" (Acts 11:26). At baptism they formally took upon themselves the name of Christ, knowing that they might well be vilified simply for bearing that name.

2:8 *really carry out.* Possibly James is here countering an argument that said in treating the rich this way they were simply obeying the law of love. His point is that if they are really loving their neighbor (and not just his wealth) they would treat the poor with equal respect. *the royal law.* James points to what Jesus called "the most important" commandment, the commandment by which he summed up all of Old Testament law. This law of love is the central moral principle by which Christians are to order their lives (Mark 12:28–33).

2:9 Favoritism is no light matter. James bluntly says that it is sin and it is lawbreaking.

2:10–13 Favoritism is not just transgression of a single law. In fact, it makes one answerable to the whole Law. The Jews thought of law-keeping in terms of credit and debit: did your good deeds outweigh your bad? The idea of judgment is connected to the need for mercy. In fact, what James is calling for in verses 2–3 is mercy for the poor. Christians are not bound by rigid laws by which they will one day be judged, as Judaism taught. So the fear of future punishment is not a deterrent to behavior. Rather, it is the inner compulsion of love that motivates the Christian to right action.

2:12 *the law of freedom.* Judaism had become encrusted with countless rules that bound people. Christians had only one principle to follow: to love others freely as Christ freely loved them (1:25; 2:8).

SESSION 5
Faith and Works
SCRIPTURE JAMES 2:14–26

Last Week

In the session last week we discussed the importance of Christians treating each other without favoritism, and really carrying out the "royal law" of loving our neighbors as ourselves. Today our session will cover the relationship between faith and works.

Ice-Breaker   15 Min.

CONNECT WITH YOUR GROUP

LEADER

If you have a new group member today, remember to do all three Ice-Breaker questions to help your new member get acquainted with everyone.

It is always a disappointment to discover that something is not as wonderful as it seemed on the surface. Enjoy getting to know one another better now as you answer the following questions about your own experiences with such disappointments.

1. What product have you purchased that just didn't live up to its advertised claims?

2. In the past, have you ever tried to appear to be someone you are really not? What areas of your life are you most likely to exaggerate about?

3. What person do you know who seems to really live up to what he or she preaches?

READ SCRIPTURE AND DISCUSS

Often it is easier to "talk the talk" than it is to "walk the walk." Read James 2:14–26 and see how important the connection between works and faith is.

Faith and Works

Reader One: [14]What good is it, my brothers, if someone says he has faith, but does not have works? Can his faith save him? [15]If a brother or sister is without clothes and lacks daily food, [16]and one of you says to them,

Reader Two: "Go in peace, keep warm, and eat well,"

Reader One: but you don't give them what the body needs, what good is it? [17]In the same way faith, if it doesn't have works, is dead by itself. [18]But someone will say,

Reader Two: "You have faith, and I have works."

Reader One: Show me your faith without works, and I will show you faith from my works. [19]You believe that God is one; you do well. The demons also believe—and they shudder.

Reader Two: [20]Foolish man! Are you willing to learn that faith without works is useless? [21]Wasn't Abraham our father justified by works when he offered Isaac his son on the altar? [22]You see that faith was active together with his works, and by works, faith was perfected. [23]So the Scripture was fulfilled that says,

Reader One: "Abraham believed God, and it was credited to him for righteousness," and he was called God's friend.

Reader Two: [24]You see that a man is justified by works and not by faith alone. [25]And in the same way, wasn't Rahab the prostitute also justified by works when she received the messengers and sent them out by a different route? [26]For just as the body without the spirit is dead, so also faith without works is dead.

James 2:14–26

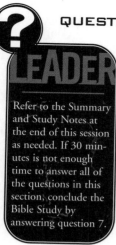

QUESTIONS FOR INTERACTION

Refer to the Summary and Study Notes at the end of this session as needed. If 30 minutes is not enough time to answer all of the questions in this section, conclude the Bible Study by answering question 7.

1. When has someone ministered to you when you were in need? When have you done the same for someone else? What did it mean to you?

2. What kind of faith is condemned in verse 14?

3. In what way is faith without works "dead" (v. 16)?

4. What kind of "works" should faith produce? Do you see the works that accompany faith in your life?

5. Verse 19 says that bare belief is not what saves—the demons believe in God, and still shudder. What is James saying here? Is salvation earned by good works, or are we saved by the kind of faith that is accompanied by actions?

6. In what way is faith perfected by works (v. 22)?

7. How should the lifestyle of a Christian verify his or her faith? What do you need to change in your own life so that you are showing your faith by your works?

GOING DEEPER:

If your group has time and/or wants a challenge, go on to this question.

8. At first glance, verses 21–23 seem to be a direct contradiction of what Paul says in Galatians 3:1–9 where he emphasizes the fact that Abraham's faith (belief) was credited to him as righteousness. What is James trying to say here? How could Abraham have been justified both by works and by faith?

♥ Caring Time

APPLY THE LESSON AND PRAY FOR ONE ANOTHER

Encourage one another in your faith as you pray and talk together.

LEADER

Encourage everyone to participate in this important time and be sure that each group member is receiving prayer support. Continue to pray for the empty chair in the closing group prayer.

1. How can we in this group support one another and help each other deal with needs in a more tangible way than, "go be warm and well fed?"

2. What needs do you have in your life right now? How can this group pray for you and help you to bear your burdens?

3. In what practical way could we as a group put our faith into practice this week?

Next Week

In the session today we focused on the relationship between faith and practice. We discussed the importance of taking action with our faith and showing that it is living and useful, rather than dead and useless. During the coming week, try to find some way each day that you can put your faith into action to help those around you who are in need (physical, emotional or spiritual). Next week we will be discussing a particularly important and challenging subject for the Christian: controlling the tongue.

Notes on James 2:14–26

SUMMARY: This is part two of James' discussion of the poor. In part one (2:1–13) the issue was discrimination against the poor. Here the issue is charity toward the poor. This section parallels the previous section structurally. Both sections begin with a key assertion which is then illustrated. This is followed by a logical argument which demonstrates the point. The section is then concluded by two arguments drawn from the Bible. This discussion of charity toward the poor is set in the larger context of the relationship between faith and works. At first glance, it would appear that James is saying exactly the opposite of what Paul taught (Rom. 3:28; Gal. 2:16). In fact, the difference is more apparent than real. The key issue for Paul is how one gains right-standing before God, while for James the issue is how one demonstrates to others the claim to have such right-standing. Paul's focus is inward. It centers on a person's relationship with God. In contrast, James' focus is outward. It centers on relationships with other people. Paul writes about how one begins the Christian life, while James writes about how one lives the Christian life. The issue for Paul is justification, while the issue for James is sanctification. Both would agree that a person is saved by Christ through faith for good works.

2:14 *my brothers.* By this phrase James signals the start of a new point. *faith.* James uses this word in a special way. The faith he speaks of here is mere intellectual affirmation. Such a mind-oriented profession stands in sharp contrast to the comprehensive, whole-life commitment that characterizes true New Testament faith. New Testament faith involves believing with all of one's being: mind, emotions, body (behavior), and spirit. The people James has in mind differ from their pagan and Jewish neighbors only in what they profess to believe. They are orthodox Christians who believe in Jesus; however, they live no differently than anyone else. *works.* Just as James uses the word "faith" in his own way, so too he uses works (or "deeds"). For James, deeds have to do with proper ethical behavior. In contrast, Paul seldom calls such behavior "works." In fact, he generally avoids the word altogether and when he does use it, he equates it to the Law ("works of the Law"). *Can his faith save him?* The implied answer to this rhetorical question is "No." This answer is based on what James just said in 2:12–13. Intellectual faith cannot save one from judgment when one has not been merciful.

2:15 *If.* A test case is proposed through which the absurdity of claiming "faith" without corresponding "action" is made evident. Though this is a hypothetical situation, it would not have been uncommon in Jerusalem for a person to lack the basics of life given the famine and the marginal economy of the area. *a brother or sister.* James picks an example in which the right action is absolutely clear. The person in need is a Christian from their own fellowship, not an outsider. *without clothes and lacks daily food.* Both are absolutely necessary to sustain life. A person without food and without warmth will die. The reference to clothes can be either to the outer tunic which was worn in public and which served as a blanket, or it can refer to clothes so ragged that they are of little use. This word can also be translated as "naked," having no clothes at all (Mark 14:51–52).

2:16 The implication is that the Christian to whom this appeal has been made could meet the need but chooses not to, and instead offers pious platitudes.

2:17 James did not dream up his conclusion here. It is what is taught consistently throughout the New Testament. John the Baptist taught it (Luke 3:8); Jesus taught it (Matt. 5:16; 7:15–21); and Paul taught it (Rom. 2:6; 14:12; 1 Cor. 3:8; 2 Cor. 5:10). *dead.* James is saying: "Your faith is not real, it is a sham. You are playing at being a Christian."

2:18 *But someone will say.* James responds to an imaginary critic who raises a new issue. This person contends that both faith and deeds are good on their own. "Some have faith, while others perform deeds. Both are praiseworthy. In either case, a person is religious." James disagrees that faith and deeds are unconnected. It is not a matter of either/or. It is both/and, as he shows in verse 22. *Show me your faith without works.* James replies that faith is invisible without deeds. If faith does not make itself known in one's lifestyle, then it is non-existent. Deeds are the only demonstration of inner faith.

2:19 James continues to press his argument. These people say they believe so he begins with the *Shema*, the central belief of both Jew and Christian: "Hear, O Israel: The Lord our God, the Lord is one" (Deut. 6:4–5; Mark 12:28–34). But then he goes on to point out that even the demons believe this (Mark 1:23–24; 5:1–7; Acts 16:16–18). They respond with a shudder because they know that God is more powerful than they and that they are in rebellion against God. Belief in one God does not automatically lead to godly action. Orthodox faith alone—which the demons have—is not enough without an obedient lifestyle. *shudder.* In certain ancient documents, this word is used in connection with magic and describes the effect a sorcerer seeks from his incantations.

2:20 *Foolish man!* "You empty man" is the literal rendering of this phrase. This was not an uncommon way for first-century preachers to address their listeners, especially when they were using the so-called diatribe style of speaking or writing. Even Jesus used this sort of strong language (Matt. 23:17).

2:21–25 James concludes by offering, via two illustrations from the Old Testament, the evidence demanded by the fool in verse 20 for the assertion that faith is useless without deeds. In both cases faith is demonstrated by means of concrete action. Abraham actually had the knife raised over his beloved son Isaac, and Rahab actually hid the spies. Without faith, Abraham would never have even considered sacrificing his only son, nor would Rahab have defied her king at great personal risk.

2:22 This is the heart of James' argument: faith and deeds working together characterize the life of the person who is truly religious. *works.* This is plural because Abraham's action with Isaac was not an isolated instance, but the culmination of many actions based on faith in God. *perfected.* The idea is not exactly that faith is somehow perfected by deeds. Rather, faith is brought to new maturity by such actions.

2:23–24 Paul uses this same verse (Gen. 15:6) to demonstrate the opposite point in Romans 4, namely that it was not by his deed but by his faith that Abraham was justified. However, Paul and James use this verse in quite different ways. Paul's point is that Abraham believed God and was declared righteous prior to the ritual action (the deed) of circumcision. But James focuses on the offering up of Isaac (Gen. 22:2,9–10)—not on the act of circumcision—and declares that this act of offering up his son demonstrated that Abraham had faith. Furthermore, the works Paul has in mind are acts of ritual law-keeping such as circumcision, food laws, and the like, whereas James is concerned about acts of charity, not fulfillment of the Law.

2:24 *by faith alone.* James is making the point that God does not approve a person on the basis of correct theology or an intellectual belief in God, but rather he approves of people who possess the kind of faith that produces faithful living.

2:25 *Rahab.* Joshua sent two spies into Jericho. Their presence was detected but Rahab hid them, sent the king's soldiers off on a wild-goose chase, and then let the spies safely down the city wall (Josh. 2:1–21).

SESSION 6
Taming the Tongue
SCRIPTURE JAMES 3:1–12

Last Week

In the session last week, we explored the relationship between faith and works and talked about what active faith should look like in our day-to-day lives. In this week's lesson, we will focus on a particularly challenging aspect of Christian character. We will discuss how we should use our speech not only to glorify God, but also to do good and not harm to others.

Ice-Breaker   15 Min.

CONNECT WITH YOUR GROUP

LEADER

Choose one or two of the Ice-Breaker questions. If you have a new group member you may want to do all three. Remember to stick closely to the three-part agenda and the time allowed for each segment.

In this section, James illustrates his point by talking about large things that are controlled by a very small part. Take turns sharing your own experiences with "steering" others, or being "steered" by them.

1. Who was your favorite teacher? How do you think you have been influenced by this teacher?

2. When have you had a lot of influence over someone else? Did you ever use this influence to get this person to help you cause mischief? Were you ever used this way?

3. In what areas do you think you are most likely to be influenced by others, either for good or bad?

   ○ Clothing.
   ○ Entertainment.
   ○ The kind of stories I tell.
   ○ How much I am willing to talk about spiritual things.
   ○ Other _____.

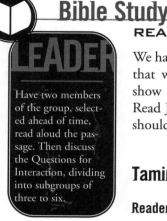

Bible Study

READ SCRIPTURE AND DISCUSS

LEADER

Have two members of the group, selected ahead of time, read aloud the passage. Then discuss the Questions for Interaction, dividing into subgroups of three to six.

We have all had experiences when we have used our tongues in ways that we regret afterwards. James uses some vivid illustrations to show how dangerous it is to misuse the gift of communication. Read James 3:1–12 and consider what he has to say about how we should speak.

Taming the Tongue

Reader One: 3 Not many should become teachers, my brothers, knowing that we will receive a stricter judgment; ²for we all stumble in many ways. If anyone does not stumble in what he says, he is a mature man who is also able to control his whole body.

Reader Two: ³Now when we put bits into the mouths of horses to make them obey us, we also guide the whole animal.

Reader One: ⁴And consider ships: though very large and driven by fierce winds, they are guided by a very small rudder wherever the will of the pilot directs.

Reader Two: ⁵So too, though the tongue is a small part of the body, it boasts great things.

Reader One: Consider how large a forest a small fire ignites. ⁶And the tongue is a fire. The tongue, a world of unrighteousness, is placed among the parts of our bodies; it pollutes the whole body, sets the course of life on fire, and is set on fire by hell. ⁷For every creature—animal or bird, reptile or fish—is tamed and has been tamed by man, ⁸but no man can tame the tongue. It is a restless evil, full of deadly poison. ⁹With it we bless our Lord and Father, and with it we curse men who are made in God's likeness.

Reader Two: ¹⁰Out of the same mouth come blessing and cursing. My brothers, these things should not be this way. ¹¹Does a spring pour out sweet and bitter water from the same opening? ¹²Can a fig tree produce olives, my brothers, or a grapevine produce figs? Neither can a saltwater spring yield fresh water.

James 3:1–12

QUESTIONS FOR INTERACTION

LEADER

Refer to the Summary and Study Notes at the end of the session as needed. If 30 minutes is not enough time to answer all of the questions in this section, conclude the Bible Study by answering question 7.

1. When is a time you put your foot in your mouth? When is a time someone really encouraged you by saying something nice?

2. Why is it such a responsibility to be a teacher, especially a teacher of the Scripture? Does the warning in verse 1 make you think twice about offering to teach someone else? Does it scare you off completely?

3. What do you think of James' definition of maturity in verse 2? Who do you know that seems to be very mature in this area? How well do you think you measure up?

4. What do the examples of the bit, rudder, and fire teach us about the importance of watching what we say?

5. In what way does the tongue "pollute the whole body" and "set the course of life on fire" (v. 6)?

   ○ Negative thoughts lead to a defeated person.
   ○ When you talk about others, you begin to believe what you say.
   ○ You can't take back loose words.
   ○ You begin to focus on the wrong things, and it is difficult to get back on course.
   ○ The words seem to slip out before you know it.
   ○ You can destroy relationships that will lead to further hurt.
   ○ Other _____.

6. What is James saying with his illustration of the sweet and bitter water and the grapevines, figs, and olives? What are some examples of harmful speech that you have seen in your own life?

7. In this past week, how much "bitter water" do you think was a part of your speech? In what ways can you make sure that what you say is pleasing to God and uplifting to others?

GOING DEEPER:

If your group has time and/or wants a challenge, go on to this question.

8. Verse 8 says, "no man can tame the tongue. It is a restless evil, full of deadly poison." In light of this, is there any hope for us as we seek to control our tongues?

Caring Time   15 Min.

APPLY THE LESSON AND PRAY FOR ONE ANOTHER

LEADER

Continue to encourage group members to invite new people to the group. Remind everyone that this group is for learning and sharing, but also for reaching out to others. Close the group prayer by thanking God for each member and for this time together.

Encourage and support one another in this Caring Time. Take turns sharing your responses to the following questions. Then share prayer requests and close with prayer.

1. In the past week, when did you experience "sweet water" from someone when you needed it? How can you pass this gift along in the coming week?

2. How can you show appreciation for the teachers in your life?

3. Are you stumbling in your walk of faith right now? How can this group pray for you?

Next Week

Today we used the lesson time to focus on the issue of controlling our unruly tongues. We examined our own lives to see where we have fallen into bitter speech patterns and discussed the importance of keeping our communications God-honoring and uplifting to others. In the coming week, ask God to help you keep a rein on your tongue and practice using it to uplift others. Next week we will discuss godly wisdom.

Notes on James 3:1–12

SUMMARY: James now shifts to his second subject: wisdom. This discussion will extend from 3:1 to 4:12. In this first section, he examines the connection between speech and wisdom. In particular, he focuses on the tongue, that organ by which we produce words, the vehicles of wisdom. Words, he says, are not insignificant. Words can be wise but they can also be deadly. The tongue is such a small organ, yet it has great power. It can control the very direction of one's life. Mature people are known by their ability to control the tongue. Certain teachers were apparently using their tongues to criticize others (and were probably being criticized in return).

3:1 *Not many should become teachers.* In the early church a person did not become a teacher by going to seminary or Bible school. None existed. Instead, teachers were called and empowered by the Holy Spirit (Rom. 12:6–7; 1 Cor. 12:28; Eph. 4:11–13). The problem was that the gift of teaching could be imitated. It was a prestigious position and if a person were eloquent, he might pretend to be a teacher. False teachers were a real problem in the first century (1 Tim. 1:7; Titus 1:11; 2 Peter 2:1–3). *teachers.* Following in the tradition of the rabbis, early Christian teachers were responsible for the moral and spiritual instruction of a local congregation. This was an especially important task in the first century since many of the Christians, being poor, would not have been very well educated and probably could not read or write. In contrast to apostles whose ministry was itinerant, teachers stayed in one location and taught a particular congregation. Teachers were held in great honor, but herein lay great danger. They might become puffed up with spiritual and intellectual pride (Matt. 23:2–7). They might begin to teach their own opinions instead of God's truth. (The Judaizers did this when they started teaching that before people could become Christians, they first had to become Jews and be circumcised—Acts 15:1–29). Or teachers might turn out to be hypocrites—teaching one thing but living another (Rom. 2:17–24). *stricter judgment.* It is dangerous to fake the gift of teaching (Matt. 12:36; 23:1–33; Mark 12:40). To mislead God's people by false words or an inappropriate lifestyle can cause great harm to those seeking to know God and follow his ways.

3:2 *stumble.* This word means "to trip, to slip up, or to make a mistake." This is not deliberate, premeditated wrongdoing. Rather, it is failure due to inadequacy. This is a problem of faulty reactions, not evil plans. *what he says.* James' focus is on words, the stock-in-trade of teachers. Thus, James launches into the main theme of this section: the sins of the tongue. It is important to notice that James is not calling here for silence, only for control (1:19). *mature.* This same word is also used in 1:4 and in 1:25, and is sometimes translated "perfect." In all three instances, it is used to describe that which is mature, complete, and whole. James is not teaching that Christians should be morally perfect, living in a state of sinlessness. This is obviously impossible.

3:3 *horses.* These huge, powerful animals can be controlled and guided by the human rider simply by means of a small bit.

3:4 *ships.* Ships were among the largest man-made objects that first-century people would have seen. That such a big structure driven by such powerful forces ("strong winds") could be controlled by so small a device as a rudder amply illustrates what James wants to say about the tongue. The person who controls the bit or rudder or tongue has control over the horse or ship or body.

3:5 *it boasts great things.* In other words, it is a powerful force and responsible for both good and evil. *fire.* During the dry season in Palestine, the scrub brush was apt to ignite easily and spread out of control. It only took a small spark to create a huge fire.

3:6 This is a notoriously difficult verse to translate and to understand. The general sense, however, is clear. The tongue is like a fire. It is capable of corrupting the whole person. Speech can burst forth into evil action. *a world of unrighteousness.* As in 1:27, the "world" is that which stands in opposition to God. The tongue is, potentially, a force for evil. *hell.* Literally Gehenna, a ravine south of Jerusalem where the garbage was burned. It became a metaphor for the place of punishment. These evil words find their inspiration and source in hell itself.

3:7–8 James pushes his case even further. Here he argues that, in fact, the tongue is basically evil.

3:7 *reptile.* In the Greco-Roman world, serpents were thought to have healing power, so the ill slept among tame snakes in the temples of Aesculapius. The modern symbol used by the medical profession has a snake entwined around a shaft.

3:8 *tame.* The Old Testament states that one of the functions of human beings is to domesticate the animal kingdom (Gen. 1:28; 9:2; Ps. 8:6–8). Yet despite our ability to control all four classes of animals (mammals, birds, amphibians and fish), we remain unable to subdue our own tongues. *restless.*

The same word is also used in 1:8 and is translated there as "unstable." It is used to describe the double-minded person. In 3:9, the dual nature of the tongue is emphasized. *deadly poison.* As with serpents, so human tongues can bring death as well (Ps. 58:3–5; 140:3).

3:9 *With it we bless.* The tongue is used in worship: praying, singing, praising, and thanking. Devout Jews offered praise to God three times a day. *we curse men.* Everybody, even James, has the same problem with the tongue. It is by means of words that people bring real harm to others. *in God's likeness.* Since people are made in the image of God, when they are cursed, God too is being cursed. The same tongue that praises God is also used to curse him, a point James makes explicit in verse 10.

3:11–12 James ends with three illustrations from nature which show how unnatural it is for human beings to use the same vehicle to utter praises and curses. Nothing in nature is like that, he says. A spring gives one type of water only—fresh water or brackish water. A tree bears only a single species of fruit.

Kinds of Wisdom
SCRIPTURE JAMES 3:13–18

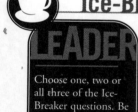

Last Week

Last week we focused on a particularly challenging aspect of Christian living as we talked about taming the tongue and keeping our communications God honoring and uplifting to others. Today we will examine the difference between godly wisdom and earthly wisdom.

Ice-Breaker   15 Min.
CONNECT WITH YOUR GROUP

LEADER

Choose one, two or all three of the Ice-Breaker questions. Be sure to welcome and introduce new group members.

Most of us would like to be wise, but sometimes it can seem pretty hopeless. Share with one another from your own experiences with wisdom—or lack of it.

1. When you were growing up, who did you think had all the answers?

    ○ Dad.
    ○ Mom.
    ○ My older sibling.
    ○ My favorite teacher.
    ○ My pastor.
    ○ The movie star I most admired.
    ○ Other _____.

2. Who do you look up to now as a wise person?

3. When you were in high school, were you more likely to think that you had it all together, or did you look for advice from people who were older than you?

Bible Study   30 Min.

READ SCRIPTURE AND DISCUSS

LEADER

Have a member of the group, selected ahead of time, read aloud the passage. Then discuss the Questions for Interaction, dividing into subgroups of three to six.

Wisdom from God is entirely different from worldly wisdom. It is characterized by very different kinds of actions. Read James 3:13–18 and see just what godly wisdom is supposed to look like.

Kinds of Wisdom

[13]Who is wise and understanding among you? He should show his works by good conduct with wisdom's gentleness. [14]But if you have bitter envy and selfish ambition in your heart, don't brag and lie in defiance of the truth. [15]Such wisdom does not come down from above, but is earthly, sensual, demonic.

[16]For where envy and selfish ambition exist, there is disorder and every kind of evil. [17]But the wisdom from above is first pure, then peace-loving, gentle, compliant, full of mercy and good fruits, without favoritism and hypocrisy. [18]And the fruit of righteousness is sown in peace by those who make peace.

James 3:13–18

QUESTIONS FOR INTERACTION

LEADER

Refer to the Summary and Study Notes at the conclusion of this session. If 30 minutes is not enough time to answer all of the questions in this section, conclude the Bible Study by answering questions 6 and 7.

1. Who is someone you admire as a peacemaker?

   ○ Our president.
   ○ Secretary General, United Nations.
   ○ The Pope.
   ○ My pastor.
   ○ My mother.
   ○ Other _____.

2. When someone gives you advice, how do you determine whether it is good or bad?

○ It depends upon who gave it.
○ If it agrees with common sense.
○ If it is unique.
○ If I have heard it before.
○ If it agrees with Scripture.
○ If my best friend likes it.
○ Other _____.

3. What characterizes the life of a person who has godly wisdom? Who have you known that showed these characteristics in his or her life?

4. What are the characteristics of wisdom that is "earthly, sensual, demonic" (v. 15)? When have you seen these characteristics in yourself?

5. What is the result of envy and selfish ambition? Where can you see the effects of these in your life right now? How can you be set free from these effects?

6. What qualities in verse 17 do you most need to develop in your life? What are you going to do about it?

7. In what situation do you need to sow the seeds of peace? How can you actually do this?

GOING DEEPER:

If your group has time and/or wants a challenge, go on to this question.

8. Verse 14 warns us not to try and cover up and lie about what is truly in our hearts. In the inside, where no one sees but you and God, which are you seeing more of in your life right now: "bitter envy and selfish ambition ... disorder and every kind of evil" (vv. 14,16) or "first pure, then peace-loving, gentle, compliant, full of mercy and good fruits" (v. 17)? Take time to examine your heart and ask God for his kind of wisdom.

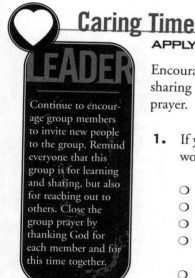

Caring Time   15 Min.

APPLY THE LESSON AND PRAY FOR ONE ANOTHER

Encourage and support one another in this Caring Time. Take turns sharing your responses to the following questions and close with prayer.

1. If you were to see your life last week on the weather report, what would it be?

○ A tornado—and my house looks like it too!
○ A thunderstorm—it has been an emotional time.
○ A warm spring day—life looks good.
○ High summer—I am basking in the knowledge of the Son's presence.
○ Below zero—I felt like God was far away.
○ Other _____.

2. How can we pray for you as you seek peace in the situation you mentioned in question 7?

3. How can we pray for and encourage one another as we all seek to develop the characteristics of Godly wisdom?

Next Week

Today we explored the difference between God's kind of wisdom, and the wisdom of the world. We looked at specific characteristics of both, and we talked about the kind of wisdom we see most in our own lives and our need to practice godly conduct. This coming week, make it your priority to seek reconciliation in any relationships that need "seeds of peace" and pray for the others in your group as they do the same thing. Next week we will be talking about submitting to God and dealing with conflict in our lives.

Notes on James 3:13–18

SUMMARY: This is part two of James' discussion of wisdom. In it, he examines how speech can be either destructive or edifying. His conclusion is that it all depends on the source of the words. In this passage, he distinguishes between wisdom from above and wisdom from below. James 3:13–18 not only looks backward to the problem of destructive speech (3:1–12), but it also looks forward to the problem such uncontrolled speech has brought to the Christian community—the issue James will deal with in the next section (4:1–12).

3:13 *Who is wise and understanding among you?* It might be anticipated that wisdom and understanding would be demonstrated by means of speech. Those who had the most understanding would possess the best verbal skills. They would be the popular teachers or the clever debaters. But this is not what James says. Much like faith, understanding is shown by how one lives. Specifically, understanding is demonstrated by a godly life and by righteous deeds. Those who truly are wise and understanding will live the kind of life that displays such wisdom. *He should show his works.* The same problem faces the Christian who has "faith," as faces the one who has "understanding." Both of these qualities are interior. Neither can be seen directly. Both must be demonstrated. As James argued in chapter two, faith is shown by the deeds it inspires. But how is understanding shown? *wisdom's gentleness.* This can also be translated "humility that comes from wisdom" (NIV). Contemporary Greek culture considered humility to be a negative characteristic, fit only for slaves and characterized by abject groveling. It was Christians who came to understand how true humility was crucial for harmonious relationships. Humble people do not need to make a point of how wise they are, and do not have to defend themselves. Conflict is defused because the humble person does not feel the need to establish a reputation of being more clever or more spiritual than others.

3:14–16 Having described how true wisdom shows itself, James now turns to a description of how "pretend" wisdom displays itself. James is concerned to show his readers that any claim to wisdom is vitiated by such behavior as he describes: it becomes a "non-wisdom." His point is not that there is a different wisdom in opposition to the true one, but that a claim to true wisdom cannot be upheld in the context of an inconsistent lifestyle.

3:14 Envy and ambition are the marks of false teachers. James is probably referring to the teachers he mentioned in 3:1 who are rivals vying for positions of authority within the Jerusalem church. Such competition clearly violates the nature of wisdom. *bitter envy.* The word translated "bitter" is the same word which was used in verse 12 to describe brackish water unfit for human consumption. It is now applied to zeal (the word translated "envy" is literally *zelos*). Zeal that has gone astray becomes jealousy. *selfish* *ambition.* The word translated here as "selfish ambition" originally meant "those who can be hired to do spinning." Then it came to mean "those who work for pay." It later came to mean "those who work only for what they get out of it" and it was applied to those who sought political office merely for personal gain. *in your heart.* This is the issue: What lies at the core of the person's being? Is it true wisdom from God or is it ambition? True wisdom will show itself through a godly life filled with loving deeds done in a humble spirit. But envy and ambition will display themselves through quite a different lifestyle (which James will describe more fully in v. 16). *don't brag and lie in defiance of the truth.* Those whose hearts are filled with this sense of rivalry and party spirit ought not to pretend that they are speaking God's wisdom. That is merely compounding the wrong.

3:15 James uses three terms—each of which is less desirable than the previous one—to describe the true origin of this "non-wisdom." There is "earthly" wisdom that arises out of this world. There is "sensual" wisdom that arises out of the "soul" of the person. Neither form of wisdom is necessarily bad, except when it claims to originate with the Spirit of God. Finally there is wisdom which is "demonic" and is not neutral. This is wisdom that is possessed by demons (2:19) or which is under the control of evil spirits.

3:16–18 James contrasts the lifestyle that emerges from pretend wisdom (v. 16) with that which arises out of true wisdom (vv. 17–18).

3:16 James now defines the kind of life that emerges out of such pretend wisdom. It is a life of disorder and evil. The logic of what he says is quite clear. When personal ambition and a party spirit control the teaching in a church, then disorder and evil reign in the community, because peace and discipline are absent.

3:17–18 In contrast is the kind of personal and communal lifestyle that emerges out of wisdom from above. Here James gives a catalogue of the characteristics of such wisdom.

3:17 *pure.* The Greek word describes a sort of moral purity that enables one to approach the "gods." *peace-loving.* This is the opposite of envy and ambition. True wisdom produces right relationships between people, which is the root idea behind the word "peace" when it is used in the New Testament. *gentle.* This is a very difficult word to translate into English. It has the sense of that "which steps in to correct things when the law itself has become unjust" as Aristotle put it. True wisdom will cause a person to be equitable and to make allowances, rather than always insisting in a harsh way on the letter of the law. The NIV has translated this word as "considerate." *compliant.* Though this Greek word can be translated (as the NIV has done, using the word "submissive") to have the sense of "a willingness to obey God," it probably should be understood in its second sense of "willingness to be persuaded," since it follows the word "gentle." True wisdom is willing to listen, learn and then yield when persuaded. *full of mercy and good fruits.* Christian mercy (compassion) is extended even to those whose troubles are their own fault and is demonstrated by concrete action ("good fruit") and not just by an emotional response. True wisdom reaches out to the unfortunate in practical ways, a point James never tires of making. *without favoritism.* Literally, "undivided"; that is, true wisdom does not vacillate back and forth. It is the opposite of the wavering person in 1:6–8. *without ... hypocrisy.* True wisdom does not act or pretend. It is honest and genuine.

3:18 Peace flows from true wisdom in contrast to the sort of harsh insistence on "truth" that divides people.

SeSSIoN 8
Submit to God
SCRIPTURE JAMES 4:1–12

Last Week

In the session last week, we focused on exploring the difference between godly wisdom and the wisdom of the world. We discussed the characteristics that mark each kind of wisdom and how we see these characteristics play out in our own lives.

Ice-Breaker   15 Min.

CONNECT WITH YOUR GROUP

LEADER

Choose one, two or all three of the Ice-Breaker questions. Be sure to welcome and introduce new group members.

We all have to deal with a certain amount of quarreling and dispute in our lives. Take turns sharing with one another from your own experiences.

1. While you were growing up, how did your parents resolve disputes between you and your siblings?

2. When it comes to dealing with conflict, do you tend to be more aggressive or more passive?

3. Which do you find personally harder to handle— an upfront noisy fight, or subtle criticism?

Bible Study   30 Min.

READ SCRIPTURE AND DISCUSS

LEADER

Select two members of the group ahead of time to read aloud the Scripture passage. Then discuss the Questions for Interaction, dividing into subgroups of three to six.

James moves from discussing the relationship between wisdom and peace to a rebuke of quarreling among believers. Read James 4:1–12 and see what James has to say about getting our perspectives right.

Submit to God

Reader One: 4 What is the source of the wars and the fights among you? Don't they come from the cravings that are at war within you? [2]You desire and do not have. You murder and covet and cannot obtain. You fight and war. You do not have because you do not ask. [3]You ask and don't receive because you ask wrongly, so that you may spend it on your desires for pleasure.

Reader Two: [4]Adulteresses! Do you not know that friendship with the world is hostility toward God? So whoever wants to be the world's friend becomes God's enemy. [5]Or do you think it's without reason the Scripture says that the Spirit He has caused to live in us yearns jealously?

[6]But He gives greater grace. Therefore He says:

Reader One: God resists the proud,
but gives grace to the humble.

Reader Two: [7]Therefore, submit to God. But resist the Devil, and he will flee from you. [8]Draw near to God, and He will draw near to you. Cleanse your hands, sinners, and purify your hearts, double-minded people! [9]Be miserable and mourn and weep. Your laughter must change to mourning and your joy to sorrow. [10]Humble yourselves before the Lord, and He will exalt you.

Reader One: [11]Don't criticize one another, brothers. He who criticizes a brother or judges his brother criticizes the law and judges the law. But if you judge the law, you are not a doer of the law but a judge. [12]There is one lawgiver and judge who is able to save and to destroy. But who are you to judge your neighbor?

James 4:1–12

QUESTIONS FOR INTERACTION

Refer to the Summary and Study Notes at the end of this session as needed. If 30 minutes is not enough time to answer all of the questions in this section, conclude the Bible Study by answering question 7.

1. When comparing yourself to others, what do you envy most?

○ Personal appearance.
○ Talents and accomplishments.
○ Personality.
○ Possessions.
○ Relationships.
○ Other _____.

2. What does James say is at the root of fights and quarrels? Do you see this true in your own life?

3. What are two reasons we do not have what we want? In your own life, is there anything that you need for which you have not asked God? What about something that you have been asking for, but that you have wrong motives for wanting?

4. What is "friendship with the world" (v. 4)? How are you most likely to fall into loyalty to this "friend?"

5. How does one submit to God? What specific actions would you take in order to submit your life to God? How can you resist the Devil?

6. When have you been criticized and judged by others? When have you done the same thing? What can you do to make sure that you do not have a critical spirit towards other people?

7. What will be the result if we humble ourselves and submit to God? How willing are you to do this? What is the first step?

GOING DEEPER:

If your group has time and/or wants a challenge, go on to this question.

8. What is James saying in verse 9? Are joy and laughter inappropriate for believers?

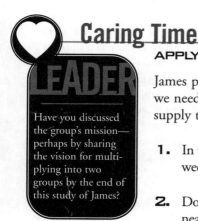

Caring Time   15 Min.

APPLY THE LESSON AND PRAY FOR ONE ANOTHER

LEADER

Have you discussed the group's mission— perhaps by sharing the vision for multiplying into two groups by the end of this study of James?

James pointed out that sometimes the reason we do not have what we need is that we do not ask. Let us take time now to ask God to supply the needs in our lives.

1. In what area of your life do you particularly need God's grace this week?

2. Do you feel God is near to you right now? How can you draw nearer to him?

3. What other requests or praises would you like to share with the group? Ask God for what you need, and also ask him to give you wisdom about things you might want.

Next Week

Today our lesson focused on some more instructions for godly living. We learned the source of discord in our lives and we also learned that the cure is to submit to God. When we come to him humbly, realizing our own sin and worthlessness, he is faithful and gracious to us. During the coming week, thank God for his grace, and ask him to help you have a humble heart before him. Particularly take to heart verses 11–12, and make an effort to not speak critically of others, even when you feel that your criticism is just. Next week we will talk about who really holds the future.

Notes on James 4:1–12

SUMMARY: The third and final part of James' discussion about wisdom has to do with life together as a church. The failure to live out God's wisdom had the most serious consequences for his readers as a community of believers.

4:1 What causes fights and quarrels among you? Where does all this strife come from? It is not initiated by the wise leaders who are peacemakers (3:18). It is not caused by persecution from the world. James is very clear that the strife is internal ("among you"). *wars and fights.* These are long-term conflicts, not sudden explosions. *cravings.* Literally, "pleasures." In Greek the word is *hedone*, from which our word "hedonism" is derived. James is not saying that personal pleasure is inherently wrong. However, there is a certain desire for gratification that springs from the wrong source and possesses a person in the pursuit of its fulfillment. *at war.* The human personality is pictured as having been invaded by an alien army. *within you.* The struggle is within a person—between that which is controlled by the Holy Spirit and that which is controlled by the world.

4:2 *You desire and do not have.* This is desire frustrated. *murder and covet.* This is how frustrated desire responds. It lashes out at others in anger and abuse. (This is probably "killing" in a metaphorical sense—Matt. 5:21–22.) It responds in jealousy to those who have what it wants. *fight and war.* But still they do not have what they desire so the hostile action continues. This mad

desire-driven quest causes a person to disregard others. *you do not ask.* One reason for this frustrated desire is a lack of prayer.

4:3 James senses a protest: "But I did ask God and I didn't get it," so he qualifies the absolute assertion in verse 2. The desire expressed in prayer may be inappropriate. God will not grant this type of request. Christians pray "in the name of Jesus," implying submission to the will of God. They can ask for wisdom and always expect to get it (if they do not waver), as James explains in 1:5. But this is different than asking for something to fulfill an illicit pleasure and expecting to get it. Prayer is not magic. The implication is not that God will not give us things that give us pleasure. God is the gracious God who gives not only bread and water but also steak and wine (Phil. 4:12). The point is that they are motivated by selfish desires and ask simply to gratify themselves. This is not the trusting child asking for a meal but the greedy child asking for the best piece. *spend.* This is the same word used in Luke 15:14 to describe the profligate behavior of the Prodigal Son.

4:4–6 To pray with wrong motives in order to fulfill one's personal pleasures is a sign of friendship with the world.

4:4 *Adulteresses!* This word probably refers to the people of Israel. By extension it refers to the church. In the Old Testament it was common to picture the relationship between God and his people as similar to the relationship between a husband and his wife (Isa. 54:5). To give spiritual allegiance to another (the world) is therefore expressed in terms of adultery. ***Do you not know.*** This is not a new teaching for them. They were aware that this was not the way to live. ***friendship with the world.*** Rather than living in God's way, in the light of God's wisdom, his people are being molded by the values and desires of secular culture. They have crossed over into the enemy's camp and decided to live there.

4:6 Their case is not hopeless. God does give grace, and repentance is possible. They can turn from their misbehavior. ***proud.*** Haughty and arrogant, to set oneself above others. ***grace.*** To receive grace, a person must ask for it. To be able to ask, one must see the need to do so. The proud person can't and doesn't see such a need; only the humble do.

4:7–10 By means of a series of 10 imperatives, James tells them how to repent. "Do this," he says, "and you will escape the mess you have gotten yourselves into." Thus, he tells them to submit, resist, come near, wash, purify, grieve, mourn, wail, change and humble themselves.

4:7 *Therefore, submit to God.* His first and primary command is that they must submit to God. It is not too surprising that James says this, since what these Christians have been doing is resisting God and his ways. As James just pointed out, it is the humble who receive God's grace. A proud person is unwilling to submit and sees no need for grace. ***resist the devil.*** Submission to God begins with resistance to Satan. Thus far they have been giving in to the devil's enticements. A clear sign of their new lifestyle will be inner resistance to evil desires. ***he will flee from you.*** Since Satan has no ultimate power over a Christian, when resisted he can do little but withdraw.

4:8 *Cleanse your hands.* Originally this was a ritual requirement whereby one became ceremonially clean in preparation for the worship of God (Ex. 30:19–21). Now it is a symbol of the sort of inner purity God desires. ***sinners.*** Those whose lives have become more characteristic of the enemy than of God. ***double-minded.*** This is the parallel word to "sinners" and expresses nicely what life with two competing masters is like. God asks for singleness of purpose in His disciples.

4:9 True repentance will often show itself in strong feelings of grief. James is not urging asceticism as a lifestyle. Rather, he is teaching about the dynamics of repentance (Jer. 4:8; Joel 2:12–14). ***mourn and weep.*** When people realize that they have been leading self-centered lives in disobedience to God, they often feel overwhelming grief.

4:10 *Humble.* This last command urges humility before God as did the first command ("submit to God").

4:11–12 James ends his section on wisdom and speech by moving from a general call to repentance (vv. 7–10) to a specific form of wrongdoing that they must deal with—the sin of judgment and the pride that underlies it.

4:11 *criticize.* This is to speak evil about other people in their absence so that they are unable to defend themselves. The word means both false accusation and harsh (though perhaps accurate) criticism. ***criticizes the law.*** When a person judges someone else, it is a violation of the royal law of love (2:8) and thus a criticism of that law because of the implicit assumption that the law is not fully true since it does not apply in this case.

4:12 *one lawgiver and judge.* To judge others is to take upon oneself a prerogative belonging only to God. God is the Judge (Ps. 75:6–7) and the Lawgiver. ***neighbor.*** The Christian's duty to his or her neighbor is quite clear. It is to love, not judge.

SESSION 9
Who Holds the Future?
SCRIPTURE JAMES 4:13–17

Last Week

Last week's lesson focused on submitting to God as the only cure for the wars and quarrels in our lives. We talked about God's grace towards the humble, and also about how we should relate to the world. Today we will be discussing how we as believers should look at planning for the future.

Ice-Breaker   15 Min.

CONNECT WITH YOUR GROUP

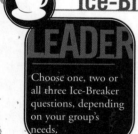

Choose one, two or all three Ice-Breaker questions, depending on your group's needs.

Some of us plan ahead more than others. Share with one another now from your own experiences by taking turns answering the following questions.

1. When you were 14, what did you think you would be doing at 24? How close to the truth were you?

2. When you travel, how much planning do you do?

- ○ I am still looking for my passport three hours before my international flight.
- ○ I always have everything arranged down to the tiniest detail.
- ○ I try to plan ahead, but I'm flexible with last minute alterations.
- ○ I don't even know whether I'm going until I actually leave.
- ○ Other _____.

3. When has some unexpected event forced you to make a drastic change in your plans?

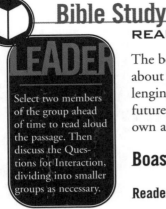

Bible Study

READ SCRIPTURE AND DISCUSS

LEADER

Select two members of the group ahead of time to read aloud the passage. Then discuss the Questions for Interaction, dividing into smaller groups as necessary.

The book of James is known for its direct, even blunt, exhortations about living out the Christian faith. In this passage, James is challenging Christians to re-think the way they look at planning for the future and making money. Read James 4:13–17 and reflect on your own attitudes, especially noticing the last verse.

Boasting about Tomorrow

Reader One: ¹³Come now, you who say,

Reader Two: "Today or tomorrow we will travel to such and such a city and spend a year there and do business and make a profit."

Reader One: ¹⁴You don't even know what tomorrow will bring—what your life will be! For you are a bit of smoke that appears for a little while, then vanishes. ¹⁵Instead, you should say,

Reader Two: "If the Lord wills, we will live and do this or that." ¹⁶But as it is, you boast in your arrogance. All such boasting is evil. ¹⁷So, for the person who knows to do good and doesn't do it, it is a sin.

James 4:13–17

QUESTIONS FOR INTERACTION

LEADER

Refer to the Summary and Study Notes at the end of this session as needed. If 30 minutes is not enough time to answer all of the questions in this section, conclude the study by answering questions 6 and 7.

1. How far into the future have you planned your life?

   ○ I have always known what I would do.
   ○ I have a direction in mind, but not the specifics.
   ○ I have a number of interests, but I want to keep my options open.
   ○ I don't have a clue.
   ○ Other _____.

2. How seriously do you tend to make your own plans for your life?

   ○ Not at all—I just make plans so I won't stagnate.
   ○ I have a really hard time being flexible.
   ○ I don't take no for an answer and push for my goals.
   ○ I don't make plans—I'd rather just drift.
   ○ I try to make my plans with my heart open to having them changed by God's leading.

3. What is wrong with the kind of planning James talks about in verses 13 and 14? What would happen in your life if you made no plans at all?

4. How easy is it for you to have the outlook James calls for in verse 15?

5. What is the boasting James is rebuking? In what ways do you think you may have fallen into this habit in your own life?

6. Take a moment to reflect on how verse 17 is true for your life, particularly when it comes to your work and career planning. When have you failed to do the good that you could have done? What is usually the reason you don't do what you know you should?

7. What does this passage say to you about the plans you are making for your future? Where do you need God's guidance?

GOING DEEPER:

If your group has time, and/or wants a challenge, go on to this question.

8. We often struggle with guilt over failing to meet other people's expectations, but sometimes this guilt is "false guilt" rather than true moral guilt. How do you tell the difference between what God wants you to do, your own natural inclinations, and what other people think you should do?

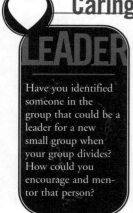

Caring Time   15 Min.

APPLY THE LESSON AND PRAY FOR ONE ANOTHER

Have you identified someone in the group that could be a leader for a new small group when your group divides? How could you encourage and mentor that person?

Recognizing that God has the ultimate say in what happens to us in the future is actually a freeing realization., it is a relief to know that someone wiser and stronger is in control. Take this time now to thank him for his care and guidance.

1. What future plans do you have that you need to release to God's leadership and guidance? Does releasing "ownership" of your future seem scary?

2. For what situation in your life would you like prayer as you seek to plan ahead with God's will in mind?

3. What special requests or praises would you like to share with the group before we close in prayer?

Next Week

Today we focused on releasing ownership of our future into God's hands. We also discussed the concept of the "sins of omission." In the coming week, ask God to help you trust him and to leave your future up to him. Ask him to point out areas of your life where you are neglecting to do the good you know. Next week we will focus our discussion on how Christians should view wealth.

Notes on James 4:13–17

SUMMARY: In verses 13–17 James begins discussion of his third and final theme: testing. He will deal with this theme, at first, as it touches the issue of wealth. He has just spoken about slander and judgment within the Christian community (4:11–12). He addresses the tensions and difficulties of wealth, both on a personal level and for the whole community. In this first part of his discussion (4:13–17), he looks at the situation of a group of Christian businessmen—in particular, at their "sins of omission."

4:13 Boasting about what will happen tomorrow is another example of human arrogance. It is in the same category as judging one another (vv. 11–12). Judgment is arrogant because God is the only legitimate judge. Boasting about the future is arrogant because God is the only one who knows what will happen in the future. Such arrogance is the opposite of humility, which is supposed to characterize Christians (v. 10), and it is also another sign of "friendship with the world"(v. 4). *Come now.* This comment stands in sharp contrast to the way James has been addressing his readers. In the previous section he called them "my brothers" (3:1,11). James reverts to this more impersonal language in addressing these merchants. *Today or tomorrow we will travel.* James lets us listen in on the plans of a group of businessmen. Possibly they are looking at a map together. In any case, they are planning for the future and are concerned with where they will go, how long they will stay, what they will do, and how much profit they will make. It appears to be an innocent conversation, the kind of conversation anyone in trade might have. But that is part of the problem: James is saying that a Christian should look at these things differently than a non-Christian. *we will travel.* Travel by traders in the first century usually took the form of caravan or

ship. There were no hard and fast timetables. Instead, one had to wait until the right transportation came along going in the right direction. However, there were certain seasons when ships sailed and caravans were more likely to travel. *do business.* The word James uses here is derived from the Greek word *emporos*, from which the English word "emporium" comes. It denotes wholesale merchants who traveled from city to city, buying and selling. A different word was used to describe local peddlers who had small businesses in the bazaars. The growth of cities and the increase of trade between them during the Greco-Roman era created great opportunities for making money. In the Bible a certain distrust of traders is sometimes expressed (Prov. 20:23; Amos 8:4–6; Rev. 18:11–20).

4:14 *tomorrow.* All such planning assumes that tomorrow will unfold like any other day, when in fact the future is anything but secure (Prov. 27:1). *what your life will be.* Is not death the great unknown? Who can know when death will interrupt plans? Jesus' parable of the rich farmer in Luke 12:16–21 illustrates the same problem. Christians need to realize that their security comes from God, not from material possessions or their own knowledge of the future. *bit of smoke.* Hosea

13:3 says, "Therefore they will be like the morning mist, like the early dew that disappears, like chaff swirling from a threshing floor, like smoke escaping through a window." (NIV)

4:15 *If the Lord wills.* This phrase (often abbreviated D.V. after its Latin form) is not used in the Old Testament, though it was found frequently in Greek and Roman literature and is used by Paul (Acts 18:21; 1 Cor. 4:19; 16:7). The uncertainty of the future ought not to be a terror to the Christian. Instead, it ought to cause an awareness of how dependent a person is upon God, and thus move that person to planning that involves God. *we will live and do this or that.* James is not ruling out planning. He says plan, but keep God in mind.

4:16 In contrast to such prayerful planning, these Christian merchants are very proud of what they do on their own. James is not condemning international trade, nor the wealth it produced. (His comments on riches come in 5:1–3.) What he is concerned about is that all this is done without reference to God, in a spirit of boastful arrogance. *boast.* The problem with this boasting is that they are claiming to have the future under control when, in fact, it is God who holds time in his hands. These are empty claims.

4:17 Some feel that this proverb-like statement may, in fact, be a saying of Jesus that was not recorded in the Gospel accounts. In any case, by it James points out the nature of so-called "sins of omission." In other words, it is sin when we fail to do what we ought to do. The more familiar definition is "sins of commission" or wrongdoing (1 John 3:4). In other words, sin can be both active and passive. Christians can sin by doing what they ought not to do (law breaking), or by not doing what they know they should do (failure). *who knows to do good.* James applies this principle to the merchants. It is not that they are cheating and stealing in the course of their business (that would be active wrongdoing). The problem is in what they fail to do. Generally James defines "the good" as acts of charity toward those in need. Certainly in the context of this letter, it would appear that these men are failing in their duty to the poor. Rather than spending all our energy in earthly investments, Jesus told us to invest in heaven (Matt. 6:19–21).

SESSION 10
Warning to the Rich
SCRIPTURE JAMES 5:1–6

Last Week

Last week we were encouraged as we realized that the future is in the hands of God. We talked about how this should affect the way we plan our lives, and we particularly spent time thinking about verse 17, where we learned that overt sins are not our only problem—there are sins of omission as well as commission.

Ice-Breaker   15 Min.
CONNECT WITH YOUR GROUP

LEADER

Choose one, two or all three Ice-Breaker questions, depending on your group's needs.

Even though we may not think of ourselves as "rich," we in this country have a degree of prosperity that would seem incredibly opulent to people in poorer regions of the world. Take turns now sharing from your own experiences with wealth before we go on to the rest of the study.

1. What rich and famous person would you most like to meet?

2. What "treasures" did you collect when you were little?

3. What is the most valuable thing you have in your purse or wallet right now?

Bible Study   30 Min.
READ SCRIPTURE AND DISCUSS

LEADER

Ahead of time, select two members of the group to read aloud the passage. Then divide into subgroups of three to six and discuss the Questions for Interaction.

We often think that "if only there was just a little more money" everything would be better or easier or more fun. Read James 5:1–6 and see what God has to say about the misuse of wealth and wrong attitudes about money.

Warning to the Rich

Reader One: 5 Come now, you rich people! Weep and wail over the miseries that are coming on you. [2] Your wealth is ruined: your clothes are moth-eaten; [3] your silver and gold are corroded, and their corrosion will be a witness against you and will eat your flesh like fire.

Reader Two: You stored up treasure in the last days! [4] Look! The pay that you withheld from the workers who reaped your fields cries out, and the outcry of the harvesters has reached the ears of the Lord of Hosts. [5] You have lived luxuriously on the land and have indulged yourselves.

Reader One: You have fattened your hearts for the day of slaughter.

Reader Two: [6] You have condemned—you have murdered—the righteous man; he does not resist you.

James 5:1–6

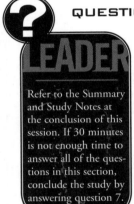

QUESTIONS FOR INTERACTION

LEADER

Refer to the Summary and Study Notes at the conclusion of this session. If 30 minutes is not enough time to answer all of the questions in this section, conclude the study by answering question 7.

1. If you inherited a million dollars, what's the first thing you would do?

2. How is success generally measured in our society? What are some of the marks of success in your community?

3. In what ways can wealth bring misery? What is James' point in verses 2–3?

4. What are the abuses the rich committed (vv. 4–6)? How do these injustices happen today?

5. What kind of "treasure" have you been storing up for the last days (v. 3)?

○ A fat bank account.
○ A generator and food supply so that whatever happens to the rest of the world I won't go hungry.
○ Treasure in heaven (Matt. 6).
○ Other _____.

6. At first glance we may not think that we can relate to the warning in this passage. How can you apply it to your situation? In what ways may you have abused the prosperity God has given you?

7. If someone looked at your spending habits, what would they learn about you? In what practical ways do you feel God would have you use your financial resources?

GOING DEEPER:

If your group has time, and or wants a challenge, go on to this question.

8. Verse 6 says that the righteous man did not resist the oppression of the rich man. Is this saying that the righteous should not resist such corrupt actions? What about standing up for justice for others? Do you think that the righteous should be activists?

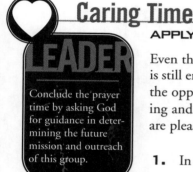

Caring Time   15 Min.

APPLY THE LESSON AND PRAY FOR ONE ANOTHER

Conclude the prayer time by asking God for guidance in determining the future mission and outreach of this group.

Even though the warning against the rich in this passage is severe, it is still encouraging to read when we realize that God does not ignore the oppressed and will ultimately bring justice. In this time of sharing and prayer, continue to encourage one another to live lives that are pleasing to God.

1. In the past week, did you feel more devoted to God or to the riches of the world?

2. What cry would you like to have reach the ears of the Lord of Hosts on your behalf right now?

3. How can this group pray for you as you seek to use your financial resources in a way that is glorifying to God?

Next Week

Today we discussed the pitfalls of wealth and talked about what God thinks of people who selfishly use their money for their own pleasure and enrichment, regardless of the needs of others. This week, ask God to show you where you have been misusing the resources he has given you, and find at least one way that you can share what you have with those who have less. Next week our lesson focuses on the exciting topic of the Lord's return, and having patience until then, even in suffering.

Notes on James 5:1–6

SUMMARY: James is still on the theme of wealth, but now he shows that riches are a great burden when seen in eternal terms. In an unusually vivid passage, James points out the ultimate worthlessness of wealth in the face of the coming judgment. Although he is addressing the rich directly, he is also warning Christians not to covet wealth. Wealth is an illusion, and it gives one a false sense of security. James tells the wealthy that riches may have been gained at the expense of the poor, even to the extent of depriving them of their. In the previous passage James was concerned with the merchant class, business people who were in this case Christians (4:13–17). In this passage, his focus is on the landowner class who were, by and large, non-Christians.

5:1 *Come now.* James continues his impersonal mode of address. *rich people.* In the first century there was a great gulf between rich and poor. Whereas a poor laborer (as in verse 4) might have received one denarius a day as wages, a rich widow was said to have cursed the scribes because they allowed her only 400 gold denarii a day to spend on luxuries! In the face of such extravagance, the words of James take on new meaning. *Weep.* James says that the appropriate response for these wealthy non-Christians is tears. Their luxury is only for the moment. In contrast, in 1:2 and 1:12, he urged the poor Christians to rejoice because their present suffering will pass, bringing with it great reward. *wail.* This is a strong word meaning "to shriek" or "howl," and is used to describe the terror that will be felt by the damned. *the miseries that are coming.* James is referring to the future Day of Judgment, an event that will take place when the Lord returns. The noun "misery" is related (in the Greek) to the verb "grieve" used in 4:9. However, there is an important difference between the two uses. In 4:9 the grieving was self-imposed, the result of seeing one's failure, and it had a good result. Repentance opened one to grace. These miseries mentioned here are the result of the horror of being judged.

5:2–3 James points to the three major forms of wealth in the first century (food, clothes and precious metals) and describes the decay of each. Agricultural products like corn and oil will rot, clothes will become moth-eaten, and even precious metal will corrode.

5:2 *clothes.* Garments were one of the main forms of wealth in the first century. They were used as a means of payment, given as gifts, and passed on to one's children (Gen. 45:22; Josh. 7:21; Judg. 14:12; 2 Kin. 5:5; Acts 20:33).

5:3 *corroded.* Pure gold and silver do not, of course, rust or corrode (though silver will tarnish). James is using hyperbole to make his point: no form of wealth will make a person immune from the final judgment. *be a witness against you.* The existence of rotten food, moth-eaten garments, and rusty coins will stand as a condemnation against the person. Instead of being stored, these goods should have been used to feed and clothe the poor. *eat your flesh like fire.* In a striking image, James pictures wealth as turning against the person and becoming part of the torment he or she must endure. Just as rust eats through metal, so too it will eat through the flesh of the rich (Mark 9:43; Luke 16:19–31). *the last days.* The early Christians felt that Jesus would return very shortly to draw his people to himself and to establish his kingdom on earth. James makes the point of how inappropriate it is to give your energies over to accumulating treasures when, in effect, time itself is drawing to a close. This is an example of the kind of arrogance and pride that plans boldly for the future as if a person can control what lies ahead (4:14–16).

5:4–6 James is very specific as he details how these people were able to accumulate such wealth. In particular he points to the injustices leveled against those who worked on the farms.

5:4 *Look!* James will not let them turn away from this stinging condemnation. They must see things as they are. They must face the reality of their own injustice. *The pay that you withheld.* If a laborer was not given his wages at the end of the day, his family would go hungry the next day. The Old Testament insists that it is wrong to withhold wages. A worker was to be paid immediately. *the workers.* In Palestine, day laborers were used to plant and harvest the crops. They were cheaper than slaves, since if a slave converted to Judaism, he or she had to be freed in the sabbatical year. *fields.* The Greek word means "estates." These were the large tracts of land owned by the very wealthy. *outcry.* This is a word used to describe the wild, incoherent cry of an animal. *the Lord of Hosts.* This means literally "The Lord of Sabbaoth;" i.e., the commander of the heavenly armies. This is an unusual title, found at only one other place in the New Testament (Rom. 9:29). James has probably drawn the title from Isaiah 5:7,9,16,24—a chapter that parallels his own in this passage.

5:5 *luxuriously.* In contrast to the hunger of the laborers is the easy living of the landowners (Amos 6:1–7). *indulged yourselves.* Not just luxury but vice is in view here. They were living in a riotous, lewd manner. *day of slaughter.* Cattle were pampered and fattened for one purpose only, to be slaughtered. On the day when this took place a great feast was held.

5:6 There is yet another accusation against the rich: they use their wealth and power to oppress the poor, even to the point of death.

SESSION 11
Patience in Suffering
SCRIPTURE JAMES 5:7–12

Last Week

Last week, we discussed James' severe warning to the rich, detailing what will happen to them if they continue in the way they have begun. God does not ignore the oppression of the poor and the injustice of self-indulgent living. The result of such behavior will be misery. The lesson today focuses on being patient until the Lord returns, even through pain and suffering.

Ice-Breaker   15 Min.

CONNECT WITH YOUR GROUP

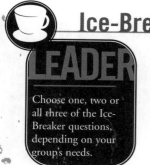

Choose one, two or all three of the Ice-Breaker questions, depending on your group's needs.

Patience is something we seem to be in constant need of, whether dealing with a serious problem or just remaining peaceful in heavy traffic and long lines. Answer the following questions about your own patience level before we go on to the rest of the study.

1. What situation wears a hole in your patience the fastest?

   ○ A long line at the checkout.
   ○ Waiting for the "dawdlers" in your family when you are already late.
   ○ Dealing with kids fighting in the car.
   ○ Trying to teach someone something that seems easy to you and difficult to them.
   ○ Other _____.

2. Do you find it more difficult to be patient over big things (like dealing with an illness, or waiting for God's timing for something you want to do) or over small things (like those mentioned in the question above)?

3. Who has been an example of godly patience to you?

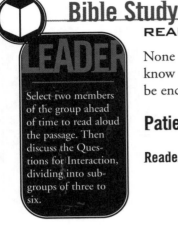

Bible Study 30 Min.

READ SCRIPTURE AND DISCUSS

LEADER

Select two members of the group ahead of time to read aloud the passage. Then discuss the Questions for Interaction, dividing into subgroups of three to six.

None of us likes suffering, but when we must endure it, it helps to know that the reward is worth the struggle. Read James 5:7–12 and be encouraged as you think about the Lord's return.

Patience in Suffering

Reader One: ⁷Therefore, brothers, be patient until the Lord's coming. See how the farmer waits for the precious fruit of the earth and is patient with it until it receives the early and the late rains. ⁸You also must be patient. Strengthen your hearts, because the Lord's coming is near.

Reader Two: ⁹Brothers, do not complain about one another, so that you will not be judged. Look, the judge stands at the door!

Reader One: ¹⁰Brothers, take the prophets who spoke in the Lord's name as an example of suffering and patience. ¹¹See, we count as blessed those who have endured. You have heard of Job's endurance and have seen the outcome from the Lord: the Lord is very compassionate and merciful.

Reader Two: ¹²Now above all, my brothers, do not swear, either by heaven or by earth or with any other oath. Your "yes" must be "yes," and your "no" must be "no," so that you won't fall under judgment.

James 5:7–12

QUESTIONS FOR INTERACTION

LEADER

Refer to the Summary and Study Notes at the end of this session as needed. If 30 minutes is not enough time to answer all of the questions in this section, conclude the Bible Study by answering question 7.

1. What event are you patiently (or impatiently) waiting for right now?

2. What are you looking forward to the most about the Lord's coming?

   ○ No longer struggling with the difficulties of this world.
   ○ Having a more complete understanding of spiritual things.
   ○ Getting to sing in a really big choir.
   ○ Being in the presence of the Lord.
   ○ Other _____.

3. How do you relate to the metaphor of the farmer waiting for his crops? What other illustration for waiting patiently can you think of that relates to your life?

4. How can you apply verse 9 to your life? How does the knowledge that Christ might return at any time affect the way you behave?

5. What kind of blessing comes with enduring through suffering (v. 11, also see 1:12–18)?

6. How good are you at keeping your word (v. 12)? How could you improve this area of your life?

7. Where in your life do you need God's help to patiently persevere? What can you do to follow the example of the prophets as they dealt with suffering (vv.10–11)?

GOING DEEPER:

If your group has time and/or wants a challenge, go on to this question.

8. How literally do you think Christians should take the command in verse 12? Obviously honesty and keeping your given word are important commands, but how far should we take the injunction to "not swear by anything"? What about taking an oath to tell the truth in a court of law? What do you see as the main point of this verse?

Caring Time   15 Min.

APPLY THE LESSON AND PRAY FOR ONE ANOTHER

Let us take this time to encourage one another in patience as we pray together for our various needs.

Following the Caring Time, discuss with your group how they would like to celebrate the last session next week. Also, discuss the possibility of splitting into two groups or continuing together with another study.

1. This past week, have you been feeling more of God's compassion and mercy, or more of his judgment? Where do you need special prayer?

2. Let us pray for the Lord to help us "strengthen our hearts" and prepare ourselves for his coming.

3. Share any other prayer requests, and close by thanking God for his promised return.

Next Week

Today's lesson was all about patiently waiting for the Lord's coming. We saw how we should conduct ourselves as we wait in readiness for him. Next week we will conclude the study of the book of James as we discuss the prayer of faith and James' closing injunctions.

Notes on James 5:7-12

SUMMARY: James' argument is finished. He has said what he wants to say about testing and temptation, about wisdom and speech, and about riches and generosity. All that remains is his conclusion by summarizing his points. However, he does not do this in a neat, systematic way. Rather, he simply alludes to each theme in the midst of offering final encouragement to the church in its struggles. In 5:7–11, he touches on the theme of trials by way of rounding off his discussion of riches. In 5:1–6 he had some harsh things to say to the opulently wealthy. Here he has some encouraging things to say to those who have been abused by the wealthy. In so doing he tells them not to grumble—this is an inappropriate form of speech. In 5:12 he again touches on the theme of speech by warning against the use of oaths. Then in 5:13–17, he returns to the idea of trials, but this time it is in the context of illness. "Pray," he says, "ask God for health." Here he interweaves the idea of speech (prayer) and wisdom ("ask God"). His concluding words in 5:19–20 identify his reason for writing the book in the first place: to bring wandering believers back to God's way of truth.

5:7–11 It has been very difficult for the church in Jerusalem. They have experience hard times of famine and poverty. Being Christians, they have received little of the general relief donated by wealthy Jewish aristocrats living outside Palestine. They have endured persecution that has pushed them down even further. When will the trials end? When will Christ return? Their hard situation has worn them down so that they are slipping from Christ's way into the ways of the world. "Hold on," James says, "stand firm, be like Job. Jesus will return." Part of this "holding on" involves not taking oaths. They are to be people of their word, not like the people of the world who abused words to get their own way.

5:7 *brothers.* James has shifted back into this personal form of address (4:11), away from his impersonal tone in 4:13 and 5:1. The atmosphere of the passage has changed from that of warning and command (4:13–5:6) to encouragement and gentle instruction. *patient.* This word (and its derivatives) are the most frequently used words in the passage. The basic idea is that of patient waiting. It is related to the endurance that James commended in 1:3 ("perseverance"), though patience connotes a more passive endurance than the active endurance of chapter 1. This word carries with it the idea of "self-restraint in the face of injustice" like that which he catalogued in 5:4–6 (having wages withheld, being used to bring opulence to a few while personally being forced to live in poverty, abuse in the courts, murder). The opposite response to such patience would be retaliation or vengeance (Rom. 2:4; 1 Peter 3:20). *until.* Such patient waiting on the part of the poor is possible because they know that when the Lord returns their situation will be radically changed. *the Lord's coming.* There are three words in the New Testament used to describe the second coming of Jesus. The first is *epiphaneia* (epiphany). It describes the appearance of a god or the ascent to the throne of an emperor (2 Tim. 4:1). The second word is *apokalupsis* (apocalypse) and means "unveiling" or "revelation" (1 Peter 1:7,13). The third word which is used here is *parousia.* It describes the invasion of a country or the arrival of a king. Taken together, these three words give the sense of what will occur when Christ returns. Jesus first came to this planet quietly as a little baby in Bethlehem. When he comes a second time it will be in great and obvious power as the rightful King. In great glory he will ascend his throne and claim his people. *See how the farmer waits.* In due course, the rains will come. In the meantime, the farmer can do nothing to hasten or delay their arrival. He must simply wait for the gift of rain. *for the precious fruit of the earth.* Likewise, he must wait for the land to give forth a crop. Once he has sown his seed (apart from pulling out weeds and keeping birds and animals away), there is nothing the farmer can do. Growth, too, is a gift. *precious.*

This was literally his most valuable possession. Without a crop he would have nothing to sell or barter, and he and his family would starve. *rains.* The fall rain was necessary to prepare the hard ground for sowing and to enable the seed to germinate. The spring rains were vital for the grain to ripen and mature.

5:8 *You also.* There is a lesson for Christians found in the experience of the farmer. They too must wait. Their fate is in the hands of an event that they can do nothing to bring about. *Strengthen your hearts.* While waiting, the temptation will be to slip into inappropriate survival modes—specifically in this case, that of adopting the methods of the world (e.g., revenge). The longer they wait, the stronger the temptation to doubt the Second Coming, and even to doubt the Christian faith itself. They must resist these temptations. *near.* The common feeling in the New Testament days was that the Lord's return was imminent—any day now (Rom. 13:11–12).

5:9 James now touches on the theme of speech. *complain.* This word is literally "groan." While groaning in the face of suffering is appropriate (Mark 7:34; Rom. 8:23), groaning at one another is not. While they wait, they are not to bicker and find fault. Such grumbling can easily develop in a tough situation in which people cannot vent their frustrations at those causing the problem, so the frustration is directed at those who are around them. *so that you will not be judged.* Grumbling against others is a form of judgment so this reference may be to the teaching of Jesus: "Do not judge, so that you won't be judged. For with the judgment you use, you will be judged, and with the measure you use, it will be measured to you" (Matt. 7:1–2). This is likely since James frequently refers to the Sermon on the Mount. Or, James may have in mind the Day of Judgment that will occur at the Second Coming. *judge.* Jesus will return to judge all. *at the door.* This is a phrase used by Jesus himself to convey a sense of immediacy concerning the Second Coming (Mark 13:29).

5:10 *take the prophets.* James does not have to mention by name all the men and women who spoke truth in God's name and suffered for it. In this oral culture, versed in Scripture, all he has to do is to make a reference and the people will think of the stories by themselves.

5:11 *endured.* At this point, James shifts from the more passive word "patience" to the idea of active perseverance under suffering, a concept which describes Job's experience. *Job.* The book of Job details the experience of this man: his illness, poverty, misunderstanding, and loss of family. Despite all this, Job does not lose his faith in God (Job 13:15; 16:19–21; 19:25). This is an apt illustration since Job's experience paralleled their experience at many points. *outcome.* In the end, God blessed Job with far more than he had at the beginning of his trials (Job 42:10–17). The implications of this are clear: if they hold on ("stand firm"), their reward too will be great. *the Lord is very compassionate and merciful.* An allusion to Psalm 103:8 or 111:4. God does not enjoy seeing people suffer, and he will intervene in the fullness of time.

5:12 James shifts back to the tongue. This is the first of a series of commandments with which he will end his letter, each of which have to do with how to live while waiting for Jesus to return. *swear.* The issue is not that of using foul language but of taking an oath to guarantee a promise. The extraordinary amount of oath taking in those days was an indication of how widespread lying and cheating was. (Honest people need no oaths.) In Jewish society, an oath containing the name of God was binding, since God was then seen as a partner in the transaction. But when God's name was not mentioned the oath was not binding. Christians are to be people of their word, not like the people of the world who used words to manipulate situations to their own advantage, finding clever ways to get around keeping their sworn word. *"yes" must be" yes".* Christians have no need for oaths. They are expected to speak only what is true. Once again, James is alluding to a saying of Jesus, who taught the same thing about oaths (Matt. 5:33–37).

SESSION 12
Prefer of Faith
SCRIPTURE JAMES 5:13–20

Last Week

In the lesson last week we focused on patiently waiting for the Lord's return, even as we undergo trials and suffering. The reward in the end will be so much greater than the suffering that we will not even remember our former pain. Today we will conclude our study of the book of James with this lesson on praying with faith.

Ice-Breaker   15 Min.
CONNECT WITH YOUR GROUP

LEADER

Begin this final session with a word of prayer and thanksgiving for this time together. Choose one or two of the Ice-Breaker questions to discuss.

Most people have strong feelings about medical practices, probably connected to the way they were brought up. Take turns answering the following questions about your experiences with medicine.

1. Which direction do you tend to lean when you are dealing with everyday minor health problems?

    ○ I rush off to the M.D. at the first sign of a sniffle.
    ○ I dose myself at home with natural remedies.
    ○ I am a natural food fanatic and wouldn't go near a doctor.

○ I am never sick.
○ I am too tough to need a doctor.
○ Other _____.

2. What is your favorite home remedy for a cold?

3. When have you been the sickest? What kind of medical intervention did you have to have?

Bible Study

READ SCRIPTURE AND DISCUSS

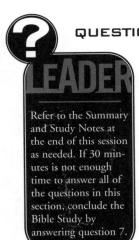

Select a member of the group ahead of time to read aloud the passage. Then discuss the Questions for Interaction, dividing into smaller groups as necessary.

James gives his final instructions for how we should behave in every situation, whether we are sad, suffering, joyful, or ill. Read James 5:13-20 and make special note of how James tells us to deal with illness.

Prayer of Faith

¹³Is anyone among you suffering? He should pray. Is anyone cheerful? He should sing praises. ¹⁴Is anyone among you sick? He should call for the elders of the church, and they should pray over him after anointing him with olive oil in the name of the Lord. ¹⁵The prayer of faith will save the sick person, and the Lord will raise him up; and if he has committed sins, he will be forgiven. ¹⁶Therefore, confess your sins to one another and pray for one another, so that you may be healed. The intense prayer of the righteous is very powerful. ¹⁷Elijah was a man with a nature like ours; yet he prayed earnestly that it would not rain, and for three years and six months it did not rain on the land. ¹⁸Then he prayed again, and the sky gave rain and the land produced its fruit.

¹⁹My brothers, if any among you strays from the truth, and someone turns him back, ²⁰he should know that whoever turns a sinner from the error of his way will save his life from death and cover a multitude of sins.

James 5:13–20

QUESTIONS FOR INTERACTION

Refer to the Summary and Study Notes at the end of this session as needed. If 30 minutes is not enough time to answer all of the questions in this section, conclude the Bible Study by answering question 7.

1. According to the responses James gives us in verse 13, is this a praying day or a singing day for you? What makes you feel this way?

2. Who is someone you admire as a person of prayer? How have you experienced the power of prayer in your life?

3. How comfortable do you feel with the idea of being anointed for sickness and praying for healing? Would the elders of your church feel comfortable doing this? Have you or has anyone you know ever been anointed this way? What happened?

4. How is confession and prayer a part of the healing process? What is the connection between the physical and spiritual areas of our lives?

5. What is the point of confessing our sins to one another? Does the idea of confessing and praying for one another seem encouraging or scary? Why?

6. What is the closest you have come to wandering from the faith? Who or what helped bring you back?

7. What has been the key thing that you learned in this study of the book of James? In what ways have you seen your relationship with the Lord grow and progress over the last three months?

GOING DEEPER:

If your group has time and/or wants a challenge, go on to this question.

8. Verse 20 refers to saving a sinner from death. Does this refer to physical death, spiritual death (eternal punishment) or something else? In what way will turning the sinner from the error of his ways "save his life and cover a multitude of sins?"

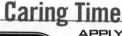

Caring Time   15 Min.

APPLY THE LESSON AND PRAY FOR ONE ANOTHER

Gather around each other now this last time and pray for one another as James tells us to do in verse 16.

1. What particular sins and struggles would you like to get rid of in your life? How can this group pray for you?

2. Is there someone you know who is wandering from the faith, that you could come alongside to encourage and turn back? Pray and ask God for wisdom.

3. How strong do you feel your faith is at this point?

Notes on James 5:13–20

SUMMARY: In literary epistles such as this one, it is customary to end with three items: an oath, a health wish, and the purpose for writing. James has each of these. In 5:12, oaths are mentioned (though not in the traditional way). James does not offer an oath to guarantee the truth of this letter. He rejects all oaths. In verses 13–18 there is a health wish, as James instructs them in how to obtain health through prayer. Finally, he sums up the purpose of his letter in verses 19–20. His aim has been to warn sinners of their erroneous ways.

5:13–18 The theme of this section is prayer. Prayer is the form of speech that James commends most highly in his letter. However, James also identifies two other forms of speech which ought to characterize Christians: singing (v. 13) and confession of sins (v. 16). Such proper speech contrasts with the two forms of improper speech identified in the previous session: grumbling (5:8) and oath-taking (5:12). In this way, James summarizes his teaching on speech while at the same time extending it to new areas.

5:13 *suffering.* James does not define the nature of the suffering. However, in the course of his letter he has pointed out a variety of troubles facing the church: favoritism (2:1–4), exploitation and litigation (2:5–7; 5:1–6), lack of the physical necessities of life (2:15), slander and cursing (3:9–12; 4:11–12), and community disharmony (3:13–4:3). He has also just alluded to the persecution of the prophets (5:10–11) and to the physical, mental and spiritual suffering of Job (5:11). *pray.* The first response to all these troubles ought to be prayer (Ps. 30; 50:15; 91:15). *cheerful.* James knows that life is not one unrelenting misery. There are times of joy and these too call for a verbal response, which in this case is singing. *sing.* The Christian church has long been noted for its singing. In his letter to the Roman Emperor Trajan describing the Christian sect, Pliny the governor of Bithynia wrote "that they were in the habit of meeting on a certain, fixed day before it was light, when they sang in alternate verses a hymn to Christ as God" (1 Cor. 14:15,26; Eph. 5:19; Col. 3:16).

5:14–15 There is a long tradition of faith-healing in the Christian church. Jesus and the apostles healed the sick. In the second century, Irenaeus wrote of healings by means of laying on of hands. In the third century, Tertullian wrote that the Roman Emperor Alexander Severus was healed by anointing.

5:14 *sick.* It is one thing to be persecuted, to be hungry or to fight with other church members. These problems stem from the evil that is in the world. But illness is another matter. It is not something anybody else does to you. What could you do? Where could you go for help? James has an answer to these questions. *call for the elders.* Illness was to be dealt with in the context of the Christian community. The elders—the council that ran the church—were to be called to minister to the ill person. They had two things to do: pray over the person and anoint him with oil. *anointing him with olive oil.* When a Jew was ill, he or she first went to a rabbi to be anointed with oil. Oil was used not only for ritual purposes but for cleaning wounds, for paralysis, and for toothaches. In this case, the olive oil is not being used as a medicine but as a part of the healing prayer (Mark 6:13; Luke 10:34).

5:15 *The prayer of faith.* James has discussed this kind of prayer already (1:5–8; 4:1–3). Notice that he seems to be talking about the faith of the elders who pray and not the faith of the sick person. *the Lord will raise him up.* James is quite clear about the source of the healing. It is not the oil, it is not the laying on of hands by the elders, nor is it even prayer in some sort of magical sense. It is God who heals. *committed sins.* Traditional Judaism maintained that there was a connection between sin and illness: "No sick person is cured of his disease until all his sins are forgiven him"

(Babylonian Talmud). In this sense, healing would be a confirmation that God had also forgiven the sins that were confessed (Mark 2:1–12). Though James does not teach an inevitable connection between sin and illness, he suggests that at times this may be the case, much as modern medicine has recognized that illness is often a product of wrong living (psychosomatic illness).

5:16 *Therefore*. James will summarize his teaching concerning healing and prayer. Public confession and believing prayer are key to what he says. ***confess your sins*.** Confessing your sins to one another removes barriers between people and promotes honesty in the Christian community. ***to one another*.** This is not an action to be taken only when one is ill or only with the elders. Public confession of sins is for everyone. ***very powerful*.** It is not that prayer is an independent force like magic incantations. Prayer is directed to God, who is all-powerful and who works in this world.

5:17 *Elijah*. Though in the story told in 1 Kings 17 and 18 no direct mention is made of Elijah praying, the rabbis taught that the words in 1 Kings 17:1, "whom I serve" (which is translated literally "standing before God") and the words in 1 Kings 18:42, "bent down to the ground," refer to prayer. ***man with a nature like ours*.** Elijah was not a plastic saint more comfortable in another world than this one. He knew depression, despair and doubt just as did the Christians in the Jerusalem church (1 Kin. 19). Still God answered his prayer in a mighty way. Perhaps James realizes at this point that he could be misinterpreted in what he said about prayer and be understood to mean that only a special few could pray and expect God to answer. Here he makes it clear that all Christians can pray like this, not just prophets or saints.

5:18 *the land produced its fruit*. In 5:7, rain necessary to grow crops is mentioned as one of the things a farmer cannot control. He must wait patiently for it to rain. Here James points out that this is not the whole story. God controls the rain and Christians can pray to him to bring rain. By implication, while patiently enduring their troubles, Christians can pray in confidence to God about them.

5:19 *strays*. Christian truth captivates not only the mind, but one's whole life, including how one lives. This is the point of James' letter. James speaks about wandering from Christian truth, presumably into other styles of living. It is not primarily doctrinal deviation that has concerned James. It is how one lives. ***truth*.** The truth is not just an intellectual knowledge of correct doctrine. The truth of the gospel is something that necessarily changes the way we act.

5:20 *turns*. This word can be translated "converts" when it is applied to unbelievers.

Personal Notes

Personal Notes

_____

_____

_____

_____

_____

_____

_____

_____

_____

_____

_____

Personal Notes

Personal Notes

Personal Notes

Personal Notes